JOURNEYS

JOURNEYS

From a Dream of Islands to Elysian Lockdown

Philip Chambers

THE CLOISTER HOUSE PRESS

First published in the United Kingdom in 2022 by
The Cloister House Press

ISBN 978-1-913460-45-7

For Jacky, Sam and Tod

I got up early so I could greet the goddess of the dawn.

BOB DYLAN, *CROSSING THE RUBICON,* ROUGH AND ROWDY WAYS, (2020).

Let the music keep our spirits high.

JACKSON BROWNE, *BEFORE THE DELUGE,* LATE FOR THE SKY, (1979).

Contents

PART ONE

A DREAM
OF ISLANDS

Bocca Della Verita

An ancient lie detector, Bocca Della Verita, made famous by the William Wyler film *Roman Holiday,* is a marble mask dating from the 13th century, its name meaning in English, The Mouth of Truth. Legend has it that it eats the hands of liars.

Early in 2011 I had radiotherapy treatment for cancer on the back of my tongue. By 2013 the cancer, I was told, would never survive the treatment. It is now 2021 and this would appear to be true. And for this I am grateful. Life is good and I am hugely relieved that the cancer has gone. But there again I never really knew I had it, in the sense that I could not see it and nor did it hurt. And when I reflect on my feelings across the passing years the cancer itself was never really something with which I had to deal. Rather it is the side effects which have significantly re-shaped my life.

Xerostomia is the technical term of what is certainly the most troubling of these side effects and dry mouth is the simple explanation of that term. Perhaps unsurprisingly, neither of these captures the complex sensations which I feel throughout my waking hours. When one experiences sensations so alien in comparison to those in a mouth with properly functioning salivary glands the isolating nature of the experience is perplexing. Perhaps it is the isolation which is the key issue and it is true to say that in the first year or two of recuperation I was always looking for listeners skilled in empathy. Despite the increasing evidence to the contrary in the political domain, it is, in my view, fundamental for humans to be able to communicate effectively and honestly with one another; and one of the finest feelings is when one experiences a real understanding with another. This for me is one of the most important human needs, allied in fact to all of the side effects which have presented themselves since radiotherapy treatment. Someone to talk to. Someone who listens. And I am happy to say I know a few such someones. In this respect the question, 'How do I feel?' may be at least partly answered by attempting to articulate what one feels and sharing it with someone else. While I regard this as a crucial, and perhaps obvious, aspect of dealing with the side effects there is something else which I discovered by chance which has helped me through the past ten years. To attempt to illustrate this the following reflective narrative centres on another means of communicating and understanding.

In September 2011 I started to write. Mostly poetry. This was not me consciously looking for connections with my emotional, psychological and physical condition. In fact, more than likely I was attempting to escape from these and from the accompanying frustrations. What I did become increasingly conscious of was how, in writing poetry, one needs to find the 'inner voice' to help one to articulate how one feels about all sorts of things. And at first these things tended to be centred on what I had noticed and loved since my youth. The natural world, birds in particular, the sea, and a feeling for a life beyond the material world; a feeling for life other than the rational.

Initially, without going out into the natural world I drew on my memories and imagination and wrote, deriving pleasure from the act of creation, from its process and from its product. Poems about birds, about feelings whilst walking, about the River Tyne, about the North Sea and about my friends and relatives began to flower. Looking at some of the products after the first couple of years writing I began to recognise some early involuntary articulations of how the effects of the treatment had become part of my changing persona, sometimes masked, sometimes providing glimpses of my search for self. A section of a poem dealing with the changing mood of the sea may serve as an example:

> The sea sings a song, the waters' rage risen
> from a peace that passes all understanding,
> the gaping mouth in its soaring and urging,
> in its surging and roaring, choked with foamy brine.

Reading this around two years after it was written, I could recognise something going on, of which I was not fully conscious at the time of writing. Apart from the satisfaction derived from writing there also appeared to be some sort of therapy at work. I subsequently wrote another poem about the River Tyne flowing into the North Sea and imagining the working men as spectres being delivered into a kind of Utopia. And still it seemed to be as much about my mouth as about anything else:

Into the salt throat, silent as the gull that glides,
hear the howls of the hosts on the Black Middens' banks.
In waves the welders, rivet heaters, catchers,
caulkers and burners, platers, joiners, plumbers
and painters, turners and fitters and finishers of brass.
Hear the choir in full spate, see the sparkles that flash
Watch the water abate as the mouths fill with ash.

Some of the writing unintentionally replicated the confusions in the behaviour of my mouth as I moved through phases of the mouth being full of salt to extreme dryness – now I know what parched *really* means – and the frustration of not being able to quench one's thirst.

But how do I feel? Well, it's complicated. The condition of the mouth still frustrates and annoys. Eating and drinking are no longer favourite pursuits. And yet .... There are the words. In words it's as if I have another sort of food, another sort of drink.

Following the initial drive to write, my subsequent reading journeys along the sea roads and islands of *The Old Ways,* opened up yet another world, a dream of islands, which, from Bardsey in 2016 to the Isle of Wight in 2019, was turned into reality. But what I could never have imagined was how the cumulative effect of sowing and reaping a wealth of words through reading and through writing, would extend beyond the pleasurable and therapeutic into experiencing and recording a range of lived experiences which would also eventually help me through the pandemic of 2020-21, transforming it into what became, for me, something of an Elysian lockdown.

ECLIPSE

Father and son were watching out of the kitchen window at the rear of the house. The son was in his father's arms because it was early morning and quite cold. But this was also because the father realised that this would ensure that his son would enjoy an uninterrupted view over the back garden and the roof of the garage. When they had come, hand in hand, down the main staircase they turned away from the front door and took the five steps down to the kitchen, after looking into the big mirror at the foot of these steps. Each then carried an image of his separate self into the kitchen, but as soon as the father picked up his son and they were able to hold onto each other, they relaxed as if into one. For twenty minutes they had watched the sky in a somatic union. Together they had shared without words, something which neither of them understood, something in which no knowledge, other than the knowledge of feeling, was at work. After the twenty minutes had elapsed, and as what I learned to call the moon was passing into the shadow of the earth, the father felt his son stir in his arms.

Opposite the kitchen door which father and son entered was another door into a cloakroom under the main staircase. Every family member accepted that for three months of the year this was a place of darkness, not of light. It may even be said that this was something of a sacred place. Each October pots of compost containing hyacinth bulbs were placed there to provide gifts and a fragrance that, even as the son's life was fading into forgetfulness, still conjured up Christmas. Over the years that followed, the same mirror into which father and son had glanced, witnessed the growth of the son, while the gloomy cloakroom became a haven for the budding boy. To the growing child that corner with the cloakroom and the mirror provided the means to reflect and be reflected as his fortunes waxed and waned. When not in use as a retreat for self-interrogation the cloakroom functioned as such spaces were intended to function. At the age of fourteen it was an ideal place to deposit the trousers from my dogtooth check suit and to slip into Wrangler jeans. This much more acceptable mode of dress, in the not so salubrious circles in which I now chose to move, was reflected in the mirror just before I left the house. Since passing the eleven plus and attending the local Grammar School, two of the three pursuits, which were my life in the later years of junior school, had now been replaced by chasing lasses. Bobby and the Whispers were the band which accompanied this activity at the Crown on a Saturday afternoon. These Saturdays were my *Days of Heaven* and a far cry from Jean Heilbron's, a Dance Academy by day, transformed from 6.30 until 8.30 on a Friday evening, into an early incarnation of a very tame Disco Fever. Any chance of shenanigans on these Friday evenings was spoiled by Jean Heilbron's torch, employed to shine on rogue snoggers in the foothills of discovering the pleasures of mutual exploration. None of this maternal policing, however, was in evidence at the Crown on a Saturday afternoon. Opposite the Savoy in Ocean Road, once the

5

innocent location of the ABC minors, the Crown offered an escape from the romantic mist of early adolescence and the promise of more serious mountaineering. The days of letters addressed to 'My dearest darling' and signed 'Your ever-loving sweetheart' were in my past. The culture that the Crown and Bobby and the Whispers opened up was one in which the lasses enjoyed frank discussion on the virtues of the terpsichorean art. 'He does it like he dances' is an observation that still has considerable resonance. As does the escape clause from inhibition which some of the lasses of a Catholic persuasion found in the form of confession.

And so football and train spotting went the way of all flesh. The trainspotting adventure had been stymied when it was clear that diesel locomotives would soon wipe steam engines off the map. Although apparently cleaner, how could Bo-Bos and Co-Cos, DMUs and even the mysterious thrumming of twin-engined Deltics compete with Streaks, Black Fives and green liveried steam engines with names like Hal o' the Wynd, Archibald Sturrock, Wolf of Badenoch and Madge Wildfire? And as for football, the days of runs down the left wing or scoring direct from a corner were over. I never forgave Mr Coggan, aka Alma Cog, the geography teacher and supposed football coach, who couldn't even see that I was the only one on the pitch who could kick with both feet. As for the third pursuit, that was currently in a significant state of flux. Birds' nesting was another matter altogether. Under the tutelage of a much wiser man than Alma Cog, birds' nesting was undergoing a transformation into bird *watching*.

Segged brogues strike parquet floor and throat is noisily cleared as the corridor echoes his presence. Striding through the open door he takes his seat on captain's chair. In trousers of cavalry twill and Harris tweed jacket, leather patches on elbows, he waits for silence. It quickly comes, for this is a man who commands respect. The group of VIth form boys are now the ones who wait as he opens the register on the desk at which he is seated. Placed on a podium the desk raises him just above the level of the pupils. With flick of wrist and folk singer's finger placed in ear, he's in a state of readiness for his performance. He recites Portia's Quality of Mercy speech then utters the familiar mantra 'marvellous boys, marvellous' and the business of the morning continues with registration.

This was a man, affectionately known as Basher Grey, to whom the love of poetry was an intuitive given. Sometimes he was the melancholy Jacques, living the Seven Ages of Man, or Oberon, who knew 'a bank

6

where the wild thyme blows.' Through him we shared with Keats 'a beakerful of the warm South … with beaded bubbles winking at the brim,' or else played tennis with *Miss Joan Hunter Dunn*. He took us to Eliot's *Waste Land*, and to smell the fish dock, the mown grass and 'the reek of buttoned carriage cloth', on the train with Philip Larkin.

Basher Grey. His broken nose and cauliflower ear tell a story of another of his loves. A pugilist in his army days. But also, a lover of the ballet, who found another sort of poetry in Nadia Nerina's interpretation of Frederick Ashton's *Sleeping Beauty*. However, it was the natural world, especially birds, which was his raison d'être. Empathy was the watchword of this Renaissance man. Imagine him as he unlaces his brogues to stand in the shoes of Shylock, or listen to him in the here and now, in a flight of fancy.

Mentor and mentee, Basher and I, along the middle reaches of the River Teme, into the steep, slanting forests of Weyman's Wood and Witchery Hole, through the lanes and shadows of a splendid autumn day, running together as stags or flying over the mountain on the wings of eagles, bright leaves still on the trees. The springtime of my life.

all a mystery Woodbury Hill under gilded sun canopies where gold dipped needles and seedful cones of larch hang temptingly and richly reflect for the red and green crossbills a carpet of beech leaves as we big spring-inspired buzzards mew and play over the canopy until bolder fitter leaner we wing our way from blue above down down into golden world to sing out fables of the brakes of bracken and hawthorn launched into the beyond no horizon to limit our horizons catapulted in this present moment out of enclosure into the future a place to establish territory and sing inheriting habitat of broom without bloom scrub thorny shrub nettles and bramble in tight narrow flight we fly these early days of living on the wing a good hiding place is vital so here we are with reed warbler and lark sounding in the ether like them unseen and like them survivors determined to be heard in dominions beyond the brakes some days we watch rook-flocks riding air plummet to feed on fields of stooks in company of jackdaws while we carrion crows annex the sacred parliament until the until primeval still in present moment I am now ardea cinerea eyes hunting bill stalking striking with such success that all will believe the mystery of the magic oil attracting fish to my heron's feet this oil young Siegfried says and Siegfried would not lie will fishermen mix with their bait and like casting their net on the other side enhance catch rejoice in musics of seed pods and seeds mosses lichens thistle-down cobwebs into the

common each day I fly only until I explore the known world mystery of all
my mission as Noah's dove firmament flying in flight divining making my
way singing forever a song of the earth a song of the sea a song of the sky
singing out my song of songs

On a walk by the Severn I lift my four-year old son, Tod, and seat him
where he can have a clear view of the river disappearing into the distant
woodland, forming from its sumptuous foliage, a naturally sculpted
carapace of trees along the horizon's bow-bent curve.

'Is that the world dad?' he asks.

BARDSEY PILGRIM

WATER

The crossing looks suspiciously like a millpond. Until the swell strikes,
lifting and dropping, unnerving and thrilling; from dry land delivered,
caressed by sea's currents, I give myself over to its ebb and flow; release
myself into its suck and pull, its rise and fall. Invigorated I master it,
accepting its embrace. Through the grip of my feet and the lived moment
of the motion of my body, it enters me.

Ignored by guillemots driven relentlessly along their flight paths, but
scrutinised by an Atlantic seal, eyes and nose just out of the water, we land
at the bay on Bardsey, off-load as a team and set foot on the island. I enter
Carreg Bach by a red door, red framed windows on either side. Croeso says
the door-mat on entry. Robinson Crusoe crosses my mind. A stroll along
the ash path which is the main road on Bardsey, takes me past the
Methodist chapel, chosen by the islanders over the option of a harbour.
This choice of a spiritual harbour as opposed to a physical one seems
apposite on an island which was, in the fifth century, a refuge for
persecuted Christians, and in the Middle Ages a place where the pope
decreed three pilgrimages as of equal benefit to the soul as one to Rome.
Adjacent to the chapel are the ruins of St Mary's Abbey, built under the
guidance of Cadfan, the Breton Saint, invited by the King of Llyn, Saint
Einion, to move to the island in about five hundred and sixteen AD.
During the centuries that followed it became known as The Land of

Indulgences, Absolution and Pardon, The Gate to Paradise, and The Road to Heaven. Earlier, thanks to Colin the boatman's navigational skills, we had taken the sea road from Hell's Mouth and steered clear of the Devil's Ridge, in order to complete the journey to Bardsey. My journey continued with a walk along the west coast, between the Irish Sea and one of the grass-covered earth banks. These are the old field boundaries, many of them riddled with rabbit burrows and providing nesting sites for the Manx shearwater, the emblem of the island, birds which only come from sea to land in order to breed. They visit after dark. But now, in the unclouded clarity of the island light, the path along the coast provides opportunities to see the wheatear perched with perfect posture, often in an elevated position. This sleek and slender bird will show you his black eye-liner in stillness, or his white arse – the meaning of his name revealed to a class of unbelieving boys by Basher Grey – as he flies away. The whimbrel too, smaller cousin of the curlew, put in regular appearances during this first encounter with the island. Meadow and rock pipit also popped up frequently in this terrain which embraced both pastures and rocky shore. But the sound which defined the island was the piping of the red-billed, red-eyed, pink-legged oystercatcher.

After my initiatory walk, Sian the warden explained the house rules and opened the door to my throne room. A spacious area, adjacent to the cottage, with an elevated closet where hay performed the same function as water.

Water. A precious commodity on the island. Well water for drinking purposes once the ritual of boiling and filtering has been undertaken. Rain water for washing.

Eleven p.m. and I'm sitting in the garden. Utterly quiet. Until the auditory assault. My imagination races as birds fly overhead in all directions; to the sea, from the sea, up and down the hill behind Carreg Bach, grandly known as the mountain.

Moon Birds

Sit in the garden in stellar beauty
stars spilling over the edge of the world,
but for the endless kiss of waves,
hushing and stilling.

Hear the pleadings cut through
darkening sky, as white in torchlight beam
spectral pilgrims bank and glide,
in tortured prayer

ebbing and flowing, their breathy
utterances choked. The moon is down
but in lunar beauty these birds
they wax, they wane,

in waves they come, moon birds
white, in flight divining making their way,
from sea to land and back again
shearing the water.

ORIENTATION

The conservation of water, demanding a carefully planned and integrated
system, on this, my first morning in Bardsey, proves a saintly task. Having
to deal with the cleansing of the body, the preparation of breakfast, and
the washing up afterwards does not only take time. Patience is also a
crucial factor when one is performing all of these duties in a limiting and
unfamiliar environment. Over breakfast I decide I should like to go and
visit the seals. This objective is held up a little longer in that, as I step out
of the door, I hear the calling of a cuckoo immediately opposite Carreg
Bach. There are five fields between me and the sea as the crow flies. The
fields, seemingly open, are separated from one another by the old grass-
covered earth banks. Or by fences. Wandering this maze does not take me
to the cuckoo, so I carry on my way to the seals, with thoughts running
through my head of how this cuckoo, heard but not seen, behaved in a
manner contrary to that which my Nana, always jokingly, applied to 'little
children,' who, she said, 'should be seen and not heard.'

Fragments

Glimpsed in the past, pressing into the present,
warm breath stirs embers into dancing flames.
Moments, fragments, a patchwork without pattern,
out of *Ashes and Diamonds*, breathing into flowering life,
my song is sung.

Was that really a fox which hung round her neck
and did the hat pins hurt when they stuck in her head?
My Dad's Aunty Emma demanded respect:
we visited *her* in her bed!
The dull bonging of the mantle clock reverberates
to warm the front parlour as Uncle Patty heaps coals
on fading embers then resumes his tireless role as fireguard,
and I, with foolscap paper before me,
frustrated once more in my efforts
to draw the sailing ship her first husband commanded,
turn to the two coveted sentinels supporting the sideboard;
but listen, she's knocking with walking-stick
on the floor of the bed-room she captains above;
a signal in Morse code, to say
she can't reach the gazunder.

I'll tell you the story of Jack and the Glory
If you don't speak in the middle of it.

In flannel combs, without a care,
he sharpened his cutthroat on strop,
while every May, on Cup Final day,
a tin of Horlicks tablets we'd share,
from the corner chemist's shop.

'Sinclair', she shouts, but he's lost among his lupins-long,
and preposterous pom-pom dahlias, as flickering fingers
delve into gloriously trumpeting nasturtiums,
and, with well-practised prestidigitation, he reveals
the black and yellow caterpillars, lying beneath the leaves;
my task of luring him once again in tatters.

His captive now, he shows me his climbing roses,
how they cling to the wall, then fall
into the back yard to lie,
with Sleeping Beauty,
in the ruins of this man's imagination;
my Granda, a pitman; and what a traveller!
The Somme, Passchendaele, Gallipoli.
My Granda slurped tea from a saucer,
spat in the fire,
and never forgot how Churchill
sent the troops into Tonypandy
against the miners.

Damp newspaper on a six-inch nail
driven into distempered wall;
mangle and poss-stick, blue bags and starch,
something still smarting stored deep in his heart.
Sometimes with tilt of head or turn of back,
he told me not to ask. Now,
at the door of a nursing 'home' he stands,
the food he picked up in despairing hands, bleeds
through fists clenched fast, as away she walks,
his pleading fingers tightening around her heart.

To bed, to bed, says Sleepy-head,
Tarry a while, says Slow,
Put on the pan, says Greedy Nan,
Let's sup before we go.

Nana always enjoyed 'a bit sit,' but not for very long;
'This won't buy the bairn a new coat,'
signalling the onset of feats of derring-do.
And here she is, seated on sill, thighs guillotined
by sliding sash, or genuflecting
as she shines the stone-step cardinal red,
then bakes cheese straws, *divine* snow cake
and coconut haystacks, in the oven at the top of the stairs.

In my Nana's house there was really only one room,
but her heart was as big as a mansion.
She prepared the table in the presence of the family,
and our cups overflowed.
Perhaps that's why Granda drank out of his saucer?

At the top of the table he sat, with Dad and Uncle Jack.
Uncle Jack liked Sabrina and he would do falsetto
on Bobby Darin's, 'Things.'
Cold cuts the comestibles for these three kings,
while we wretched ones, below the salt,
dined on the Sunday serial;
shared the stolen loaf with Jean Valjean
and the savoury pie with Abel Magwitch.

All attended by our very own grisettes,
Nana's girls: Mam, Aunt Emmy,
and Marilyn the younger,
if she hadn't stormed out in a fit of pique,
and locked herself in her bedroom
with the kidney-shaped dressing table
and the vanity set.

Now Nana's reaching into the back of that cupboard.
Must be sweetie time.
A Dainty Dinah toffee or the one with the begging dog?
'It's too good for you Spot!'
Adults first, but the tin is getting closer.
Don't get this wrong. Which one will it be?
Wait a minute, I haven't seen those ones before.
My Nana.
Held my face firm in her hands,
kissed me on the lips,
said she was weary.

Clap your hands for daddy coming down the wagon way,
Pockets full of money and his hands all clay.

Shrouded in steam he exits from his ablutions,
and the bathroom weeps condensation, while into hallway
he steps, smacking his face as Old Spice lotion stings,
and he loiters and sings, a song of Richard Tauber.

'One alone, to be my own, I alone, to know her caresses,
One to be, eternally, the one my worshipping soul possesses.'
A pack of Parma Violets and a King Edward half corona
in the car. 'To see a man about a dog,' his destination
he tells me, returning only with beatific brandy smile
and best bitter beer on his breath.
My Dad invented Friday nights out.

Once upon a lovely life ago,
with Brylcreem sheen and Woodbine taint,
that man Tommy Bulley served up the rations
as on the Co-op counter I sat, in a world
of broken biscuits and shipshape cheese.
That man had only three fingers on one hand.
Cut one off on the bacon slicing machine.
Me Mam told me.

Night, night,
Sleep tight,
Hope the bugs don't bite.

The seals were in their safe haven, amongst seaweed and rocks, or in the water, when I arrived. Individuals with their own storied history.

Seals in Seals' Clothing

On kelp, on wrack, bladder and serrated,
or in their salty, supportive element
the seals disport themselves.

These seals are stamped with selfhood,
one seduces the sailor in me, as she
combs her imagined hair.

Another looks at me through sad, watery
eyes. Yet another shuffles off
his rocky roost, flaunting

his prowess, oh so at home in the water;
in the seconds it takes to swap
land for sea he has evolved.

Now he's on song, shining in his element,
while on land it seems
a furriers has been raided.

White mink, astrakhan, ocelot, tortoiseshell,
polar bear, Arctic fox. Surely it's faux fur?
That one next to the white mink is making
quite a statement. Like Hil and Bill, up
to the minute in brushtail possum.
'Eco-fur' I'm told.

I sit outside with Dave from the Wirral, on what is still a cold day, so cold that I had called on my surprisingly unforgotten fire-lighting skills early that morning. Three barn swallows in their highly favoured habitat of farmland search with dizzying swoops for insects as I tell my story of the Manx shearwater under the star-filled sky, and we agree to meet that night at ten-thirty to have a look at these birds on another part of the island known as the Plantation. This is on the northern headland close to the sea and the ruins of the Abbey.

I return to the welcoming red door and the croeso-captioned door-mat and an equally welcoming smell of wood-smoke in the croglofft cottage. Smug with the success of my fire-lighting skills I call on my culinary skills by boiling two eggs.

I watch from the window as the mist rolls in, the wood-smoke smell soothing and dulling, the muted piping of the oystercatchers tuning me in to the island, my bare feet cool on the stone floor once trod by Nathaniel and Mary Williams; and as my heavy eyes turn to the icon of Wales, a print of Vosper's Salem hanging above the fire, the slight taste of sulphur lingering in my mouth, I see in the shawl the depiction of the devil.

At ten-thirty that evening, equipped with torches, and woolly hats on heads we made our way to the north of the island, past the chapel and what was left of the Abbey, to the Plantation. Here we stood next to a shelter belt of conifers protecting the oak, the ash, the wych elm, the Italian alder and the blackthorn that made up the plantation proper. Under a virtually starless and misty sky we waited for the Manx shearwater to take the stage. Out at sea they would be rafting up and moving inshore. The mist did not retreat as the evening slowly advanced, but after about twenty minutes we heard at a distance the first demented calls. As the calls came closer we caught sight of the white underparts of the occasional bird. Five minutes later we were able to hold the birds in beams of light. There were not the numbers of the night before. Or perhaps it was simply that we could not see the huge numbers under their favoured cloak of darkness, darkness which was becoming inkier by the minute. This provided a cue for Dave to take the path homeward to the Observatory where he was staying.

Back in the croglofft cottage I climb up the ladder to my bed in the loft, a ladder ascended and descended in the nineteenth century by Nathaniel and Mary. Cocooned in a twenty-first century sleeping bag I smile myself to sleep.

Headstone Inscription in the Abbey Graveyard:

ER COTH AM*
NATHANIEL WILLIAMS, AGED 80
1895
Hefydsibriod**
MARY WILLIAMS, AGED 89
1907
Of Carreg Bach, Enlli
Footstone Inscription in the Abbey Graveyard:
NW
MW

*In memoriam   ** Also his wife

BREATHLESS WITH ADORATION

As I replenish the bucket with rain water from the water butt at the foot of the mountain the reeling of a grasshopper warbler pervades the air on this cloudless morning under an azure sky, more reminiscent of summer than of spring. Like the cuckoo the grasshopper warbler heard but not seen. Through the paddock freshly ploughed, and through the gorse to the north end of the mountain looking down on the plantation of oak, ash, elm, alder and blackthorn as I travel up. Next to my feet a green-veined white, the commonest butterfly on the island, and nearer the summit a lost lamb calling to its dam. A pair of ravens, oily, ebony sheen in sunlight, loud cries resonating through the otherwise silence. I have brought the folding camp chair complete with cup holder and camouflaged in green. The chair was once my mother's.

Electric Fields

Wheels turn wetly, licking the slick of the road,
rotary motion and electrical energy conspiring
now in reciprocation; contact-breaker points
set the sparks, fuel jets through needle-eye,
cam-shafts lift tappets, valves breathe,
hammering pistons, rings sprung tight,
glide smooth in cylinder. Induction,
compression, firing, exhaust,
blurred overlap all in tune
take me to my destination.

Gold-leaf light illumines the pages of fields
exhausted by the drenching of unrelenting
rain. Diluted and swollen by so much water,
every particle of earth charged with words,
conducting and resisting; earth, burnished
and scoured to shine, a mirror of itself, rain
reduced and fragile. The purged sky waits,
deliquescent air thick now
with unseen moisture;
unknowing, my mother waits too.

A network of nerve cells pulse at the synapse
junction, while in spiral wrap the myelin
sheath carries in its plasma membrane
the sodium channels and electrolyte
in a field where connectivity is all.
Conductivity damaged by dehydration,
the once perfectly timed jumps
of saltimbanques, fuse and splutter;
her contact with life
in brittle-wired
delicate balance.

Still she's with me on the mountain as I look across Bardsey Sound to the southern-most tip of the Lleyn Peninsula, swallows swooping around me as I sit in stillness.

Just Water

In crumpled suit of flesh she sleeps.
On waking, though slipping
like words beyond my reach,
she smiles a firm, glum smile
then asks only for water.

A light shines lately in her eyes.
Each morning it appears,
reminding me just how
much better is what we know
than what we never will.

I tilt the cup to quench her thirst for life.
She sips as with flute and flirty tail dip
he arrives. From trembling feathers
water drops are flung, shine effulgent,
energise air, as in her garden
blackbird bathes. I drink it in.

A little further and now I'm sitting on the summit, bare feet on the wiry ling and the slightly softer bell heather, not yet in flower so early in the spring. I bring some of the birds beneath me rather closer with the help of a telescope. A large community of mostly lesser black-backed gulls with a few herring gulls, sit uncharacteristically quietly on the higher but inaccessible grassland. Some had already built nests on the ground and would incubate the eggs, brood the young and guard them until they fledged as the grass grew around them, affording more protection.

Moving further along the east side of the island I find a spot where I can sit safely, in the by now extremely warm spring-time sun, and watch the birds beneath as they fly to and from their nesting sites on the sheer cliff face, or swim over the clear blue-green waters of this enchanting island. It takes a telescope to distinguish between the razorbills and guillemots and to recognise that the flotilla is made up of seven puffins. The telescope is also necessary to separate the cormorants from the shags but the binoculars are perfect to follow the choughs, one on its own then five together, sometimes below, sometimes above, their frequent calls of 'churr' and 'chyah,' and especially 'k'chuf,' serving to remind me what they are. Aerobatic skills have them soaring above in buoyant flight, one even coming down to settle obligingly on a rock in front of me and preen for my pleasure. One more glance through the telescope reveals two cormorants in flight, low over the pure water of Bardsey Sound. Struck then by the green sheen of the smaller shags, caught in the sunlight as two of them float over the confined deep, me up above, flying.

Bare feet on warm rock, on wiry ling, on soft bell heather. Firm earth under and sea all around. I enter all. All enters me.

I awake to take the Lord's Path along the summit from the north end of the mountain to the south. From the south end I watch a pair of ravens rolling through the air. This rolling proved only a precursor to the derring-do that followed. There's a heaviness in their functional flight which is put to thrilling use as they tumble toward the earth, fly ostentatiously upside down and nose-dive in their seeming delight. Their spring play-ground the sky, they pattern the air with their pathways.

I settle into my seat to rest before the descent. I lean back and look up. Choughs. Two pairs. Glossed blue-black, curved red bills. Bounding to buoyant in flight. Late afternoon lyricism. Adagio for strings, cleansing and purifying.

INFINITE VARIETY

Hair washing. It is worth remembering that since water is scarce it ought to be used prudently. One wash and one rinse, despite what most proprietary brands recommend, is quite sufficient. The water is, of course, rain water. If, like me, you are inclined to be lucky, you may, when collecting it from the water butt, hear a grasshopper warbler or see a chough. Regrettably you are unlikely to see a grasshopper warbler it being a retiring bird, inclined to creep through the undergrowth.

This morning is a particularly gregarious affair, especially compared with yesterday's circumambulation of the mountain top. At ten-thirty Steffan is conducting a guided walk, beginning at the Observatory.

Northern purlieus of the island shape themselves in my mind as my afternoon pathways as in the present moment of the morning we saunter south. Up behind the farm toward the south-east corner of the island to Pen Cristin, an area of maritime grassland, springy with rich turf and now yellowing with lesser celandine underfoot. Linnets, meadow pipits, pied wagtails and an increasing number of swallows further enrich this palette of colour and sound as a raven drops silently into an adjacent field.

We continue walking further up the side of the mountain, the farm shrinking as we ascend and the discussion centring on key points in identifying a raven; in flight the diamond-shaped tail and Maltese-cross appearance, up close the stout, black bill and shaggy throat. The voice a deep croak or 'cronk.' We turn our eyes to the path we are walking as Steffan points out the golden hair lichen, rare and sensitive, tolerating only the purest air. Alongside the yellow-orange, golden hair, the green-grey, ciliate, strap lichen. A little closer to the cliff edge, from which vantage point we see guillemots, chocolate brown and white, and the black and white razorbills, sailing beneath. Carrying along the coast and down to the boathouse and the bay where we landed almost three days ago, we cross the Narrows, leaving the yellow lesser celandine behind us and finding instead under our feet, patches of blue spring squill renewing itself. In conversation with the giant of a man whose passion is wild flowers I discuss whether the delicacy of the pale pastel blue might be seen as closer to the hue of indigo or violet.

Solfach beach on the west coast. We stand and look across the Irish Sea, where, on a clear day it is possible to see the Wicklow Mountains. Among the pied wagtails on the shore Steffan points out one white wagtail. It occurs to me when looking at this white wagtail, whose back is grey, that a good way of remembering the colour of wagtails is that the pied is black and white, the white is grey, the grey is yellow and the yellow is olive.

The end of the guided walk is nigh and Steffan asks if we would like to return to the Observatory via the Withies, a wetland area running down the centre of the island. This is a habitat of damp grassland, reed beds and copses of willow. Very marshy he tells us. I opt for plodging through the clarts, as does one of the ladies from Liverpool.

So Steffan leads we two along another track through this varied landscape that is Ynys Enlli, Bardsey Island, The Island of Twenty-thousand Saints, The Island in the Currents, The Island of the Bards, while the remainder return to the Observatory over the ash of the main island road.

The Withies draws me just as the sea has drawn me every day since I arrived on this magical island. I know I shall be back even before the perfect sighting of a male stonechat in striking summer plumage. Black head, white collar and orange-red breast gleam in this gorsy place as we three pilgrims of these wetlands feel our way over marshy terrain; test for firm footholds; 'make our road by walking.'

Mulligatawny soup and cheese biscuits for lunch, then, as predicted, the northern purlieus of the island become my afternoon pathways, beginning with a saunter down to the Methodist chapel. This grey Gothic building sits solid and peaceful in the green hollow at the foot of the mountain, Mynydd Enlli. Two square colonnades have helped the chapel weather well and the attention to detail in its maintenance is evidenced in the way in which all of the corners have been worked with carved gritstone collected from the ruins of old houses on the island. This is in tune with the spiritual and material self-sufficiency of Bardsey Island, further demonstrated in that one side and a gable end of the chapel are worked with limestone chiselled square, taken from the shore of the island. In perfect reciprocity the chapel is part of the island and the island part of the chapel; a reciprocity at once symbolic and actual.

Access to the chapel porch is gained through a robust double door of oak. The porch itself is floored with red tiles and leads in turn through another door of oak, and along a floor tiled white, to the pulpit. The pulpit is of old black oak with carved panels depicting leaves and fruit. This created a feeling of something Pantheistic, or even Pagan, with its emphasis upon the stark and the natural. There were, however, some complementary Christian icons to redress the balance. On a triangular panel in front of the pulpit were emblems such as the crowing cock, the sponge, the spear, the hammer and nails, all in brass relief.

The saunter continued around Nant Withy. A portion of Bardsey more Golgotha or Gethsemane than Eden or Avalon. More agony than ecstasy. Dense thickets of blackthorn, gnarled elders, coppiced osiers, withies sprouting. Smaller thickets of wild pear as if leaning away from the wind and toward the lee of the island. These small thickets of suckers create ideal habitats for secretive reed warblers. Their rhythmic song heard frequently but the bird only occasionally seen. The nets are out this afternoon in this dark corner, and Mark, assistant warden along with Steffan, is ringing warblers. A blackcap, wings spread, crown toward the earth, hangs in the net. An occasional flutter is heard in an otherwise silent moment. I leave through the thickets of thorns, scratching my head as I go.

After the sombre chapel and the dark corner that was Nant Withy I pass along colonnades of conifers to reach the broad, spreading canopies of wych elm and alder, where the light flows in and the leaflets of the sessile oaks and the elegant ash tremble with birdsong.

A walk around the periphery of the plantation and then I sit, swallows, six of them swoop round my feet. A willow warbler sings on the edge of the conifer belt. Then the promise is fulfilled. A spotted flycatcher undulates in, to the edge of the field in my field of view, and perches on post with upright posture to make his insect-catching aerial sorties. A passage migrant in these parts, perhaps toward territory unknown. With his perfect posture I am reminded of the wheatear, but whereas the wheatear is a handsome bird the spotted flycatcher is more of a pretty little charmer.

Meanwhile, back in the nineteen-fifties, a tractor is ploughing a field on the north-west corner of this journey into the past. The scene is affectingly familiar, except that the peewits have been supplanted by two-hundred gulls. Mainly herring, some lesser-black backed. Drawn to the past and drawn to the sea I walk yet again the path between the Irish Sea and the old grass-covered earth bank field boundaries. All of *The Usual Suspects* in attendance; wheatear and whimbrel, meadow pipit and rock pipit, and of course the oystercatchers. But it is the swallows who catch my eye at every instant. All along the coast numbers increasing, even as around my legs they glide, hunting for insects in the late afternoon.

TO THE LIGHTHOUSE

My route is along the Narrows to the lighthouse and then to the southern end of the island. I sit and see what I can see in the maritime grassland of the Narrows. The thrift is thriving, pretty in pink, but the spring squill is the star of Bardsey with its blue, star-shaped flowers in clusters, spreading through these grassy places next the sea. Bird's foot trefoil is not yet in flower but the triple leaflets which explain the name are not difficult to see, especially with this close-up, bird's-eye view. And the glory of wild thyme which stretches over to the sands of Solfach beach is showing tiny, pale pink flowers to the sun.

I count thirty-four seals, forty-six oystercatchers and two wheatear, before being tempted to take my seat to Solfach beach. I pause there to watch two pairs of shelduck sailing off shore as the turnstone, perfectly camouflaged in their tortoiseshell colours, feed along the line of kelp deposited on the beach at the turning of the tide.

But the fingerpost points to the lighthouse as my next port of call. And here I sit against the lighthouse wall, having abandoned the chair. Boots and socks abandoned too, bare feet caress then sink into the pile of the turf carpet. Four dunlin, coastal waders, in company with two ringed plover, away from sand and shingle. A gregarious grouping who kindly share their turf with this solitary interloper. And then they are gone. Only I remain. They have turned their backs on me, as I have turned mine on the lighthouse. I stand and turn again to give it my attention.

As with the chapel, so with the lighthouse; it is part of the island, the island part of it. The ashlar limestone, indigenous to Ynys Enlli and used in its construction, enabled the building of a square tower lighthouse since such stone can be dressed, or cut, until squared. It is painted in red and white bands. Around it are these other wonders. Two wheatear bowing and bobbing and chasing flies. The whimbrel, smaller edition of the curlew, a wader who whistles a plangent, bubbling call of seven notes descending in pitch.

Coasting along cliff edge, watching wheatear catch the wind, feeling the tilt and curve of the world, I walk the promontory, tracking the endless horizon's bow-bend. I am spindrift, wind-borne, will o' the wisp. All enters me. I enter all.

A PAEAN IN SIX POEMS

Costs/Benefits Analysis

Can words say anything? Do not words destroy the symbol that lies beyond the reach of words?

FLUSH, VIRGINIA WOOLF

Exiled by illness in a kingdom of words, words
I write to hammer out, precious as beaten gold,
the meaning in my mouth of xerostomia, trismus,
osteonecrosis, thrush and mucositis, and sweet
sounding accomplices, lymphoedema and fibrosis.
No name as yet for enamel thinning and splintering
around the shrinking dentine nor for fungal growth
on tongue, while eye-clouding cataracts also thrive
on toxicity associated with standard fractionated
radiation therapy to the head and to the neck.
A reduction in salivary output and increased viscosity
of the saliva are common early complaints following
radiation therapy. These changes, typically permanent;
collateral damage they call it ....
Flocculent, flocculent ....what a beautiful word.

Myriad-Minds

Who is it that can tell me who I am?

KING LEAR, WILLIAM SHAKESPEARE

The fingerpost points to Elvedon
though no one has been there,
there the lady sits, between two windows writing,
writing of the tides that bind, in water and in air.
One equal music murmuring, she, the thing itself,
ordering the scattered kingdom of her mind.
Limitless this mind delights her,
walking her down avenues of elms,
sitting her on ring of grass enduring;
like light through translucent leaves
transported, entering the temple of the beech,
showing time tapering toward a point;
the parallax view. There she gazes, dancing
into different perspectives,
where Rhoda seeks her face
and Jinny hoards life in her lived body.
Beauty in obedience, majesty in order
are Louis' battle cries; in his perplexity
Bernard tells stories, Susan seeks solitude,
Neville a vision. Yet how life withers
when the good minute goes,
when there are things we cannot share;
so we seek among phrases and fragments,
to find in the flame of the present moment
something unbroken.
The bells toll time's strokes, tintinnabulation cruel and kind.
Listen to sweet Virginia cry, who is it that can tell me who I am?
Fishing for the divine specific, fragments to shore against her ruin,
in the foul rag-and-bone shop of the heart,
moments of being.

The Flaneur

As silence falls I am dissolved utterly and become featureless and scarcely to be distinguished from another.

In solitude he moved, an isolate unoriented,
at first not knowing how he through her was not
in fact alone, until she joined the dots and dashes
into continuous lines, all separateness eliminating,
connecting in her myriad-mindedness, solid earth,
a liquid fit to drown a life, gaseous exchanges –
our life's breath and blood – and stars of plasma,
via that quintessential element, poetry of the ether.

And now in streets he walks with others,
never a stranger on a train or when all at sea;
and now he notices, even in thin air itself,
how one path always flows toward another.
Thus we are included, we and others; and I,
a new self, who seems now to be me.

One By Means Of Two

Then suddenly descended upon me the obscure, the mystic sense of adoration, of completeness that mingled over chaos.

THE WAVES, VIRGINIA WOOLF

In the wind the fingerpost swings,
on the page words stand still,
the world turns, the sun dies,
banners flap, dust flies, afraid
and excited, agitated aspen,
leaves tremulous, stir the air.
Terrified and beautiful
in her knowledge of limitations,
the terror and beauty in knowing
and partly knowing, the purlieus
and the provenance of our lives,
the fear and compulsion
in the limited and the unlimited,
oxymoronic hendiadyses,
undivided in their differences.

Somewhere in the certain dark,
when night falls on thoughts
goaded and garnered, who knows,
through sterile days in search of words,
words which feel and sing,
just what may emerge,
when, somewhat tripping over thoughts,
fortune falls. That newness of morning
when the story ends, somehow the song begins.

In the eclipse, myriad-minded,
the lady writes; lighter later here
she thinks, despite the darkness.

Transfiguration

I have seen my sons and daughters, once netted over like fruit in their cots, break the meshes and walk with me, taller than I am, casting shadows on the grass.

THE WAVES, VIRGINIA WOOLF

Echoing endlessly in mind's caverns
the clangorous ringing of water dripping
inhabits his head.

A drift into darkness and silence follows.
Mystery is suffocated in fields of ice.
Now in the crucible magic lies latent.

In primaeval stillness imagine another,
suspended by threads,
planes patterned in burnished magenta
thickly seamed with pitch,
furnished with armour of satin like steel,
finished with spikes.

Soft the underbelly to the touch,
visceral, swollen,
over-heated, ripe.

Out of chrysalis cracking
under pulse of sun
fused feathers force a way
through shoulder-blades' fevered itch,
in purest adagio unfolding to form
wings which are now in splendour revealed.

Eclosure completed, Pegasus blazes,
winged to master the breathing of air,
hoofed to measure earth's give and take.

Around the air he wraps his wings,
soaring in ecstasy white as love,
by crepuscular rays lifted
over fractured clouds
in dying sky incarnadine,
to fall at dawn in flight's embrace.

Now his hooves will strike the earth
and from the scars
springs of inspiration spring.

And in the sparks of this idea
his eyes at last may light upon
a being in a moment of being.

Freewheeling

**We too, as we put on our hats and push open the door, stride not
into chaos, but into a world that our own force can subjugate and
make part of the illumined and everlasting road.**

THE WAVES, VIRGINIA WOOLF

As if for first time unlocked, this life's hoard now forever open;
never empty, never ending. From Clows Top I claim Abberley Hills,
gather samphire on cliffs, cling salt sea with open arms, see 'fin'
at film's end, signifying nothing but the impossible.

Picture this piece of music I'm hearing, gathering and ordering light
through stained glass streaming, seated in cathedral, eyes bleeding;
in present moment Bach ablaze, as sea swells full-flood, head high
a feathered breast stirring, so soft its vermiculations,

or the time Richard Tauber sang Adieu Mein Kleiner Gardeoffizier
and my father listened, sprawled, leg over arm in chair of choice;
the cynosure, the sure sign, the thing itself, only itself.

Singing against the sky, hills' silhouettes, a key signature signifying, repeating their patterning into infinity, the familiar falling away, fleet and fugitive, as car now climbs where once I climbed.

Neutral selected, now I coast, bouncing off tightly curved corners to straddle double white lines, once sacrosanct; as Jerseys graze, magpies blur and sheep safely gaze.

In sunlit solitude singing, bleached back into another time, in my chariot I fly. Reflected in the windscreen I see a bird caged in car and feel the skull beneath the skin.

Now it's downhill all the way. In freefall, portal opens wide, and with wings sprouting from head and heels I am become Hermes, flying into a subterranean utopia.

Into this mountain, to front the facts of life I fly; though I cannot eat my dinner yet I know this island's mine, and I, and I, and I again, will beat forever this air with wings.

At the end of the promontory I sit with the oystercatchers. I, another sentinel looking out to sea. Wheatears look too, proud in upright posture. I look with them and the seals they look at me as the choughs' fingered wingtips feel the air, a fine caress; and invisible now at sea, gannets glide and soar then fold their wings to plummet through clear air and into water, while wings held stiffly, moon birds shear the waves.

As predicted I return to the Withies. This time, before making my road over the wetlands, I conduct a seated reconnaissance. At first the sound which is becoming another island identifier as my days here pass the half-way mark. A sudden burst of song, loud and warbling, ending in a trill. Next, a song less vehement and energetic than the first, but a familiar warbling sound. Then a descending song, a song sung in flight and starting and ending on the ground. Finally a colourful medley of twittering notes delivered from a perch. These are the songs of three small brown birds I listen to as I sit. Wren, dunnock and meadow pipit. Along with the blushing linnet.

Readying myself to continue the reconnaissance on foot another brown bird, or brownish-black, but not small, rushes through the air on scimitar wings. A devil bird on The Island of Twenty-thousand Saints. It's also the first swift I have seen this year.

Into the Withies to make my marshy road. Through greengold gorse and wild watercress in ditches, I weave my way. Marshy terrain forces me round a circuitous route to the osiers I aimed for, then the duckboards deliver me the kingcups, huge and brilliant gold, their loving leaves envious glossed hearts, lighting up the dark places at the edge of the walkway of this wetland world.

At the end of the cul-de-sac a crow's nest tells me why there are no other birds nesting in the vicinity. I retrace my steps to where the duckboards begin. Standing for a moment to decide my next direction I hear the sound of the wind in the Withies. The marsh woundwort will not be seen until July, but the odour of leaf-mould on the breeze betrays the presence of last year's decaying leaves. I strike north. A flock of around twenty linnets dance through the air, twittering, on their way from the Withies to a favoured feeding ground on fields of pasture. I follow their lead, listening as I saunter, to the fifth singing wren of the day. Once out of earshot a female stonechat takes over, commanding my attention from her prominent perch on fence-post, then, with flitting flight leads me to a gate on the edge of the pasture. A lone chough flies toward the sea. I resist the call, being drawn instead to the Plantation.

Many swallows on the island now, and at this northern point, adjacent to the sea, about twenty glide easily, skimming about my feet. Gulls, sitting high on the thermals, soaring and coasting singly; and a pair of carrion crows, so high 'I would have broke mine eye-strings, cracked them' to see.

PLANTS AND BIRDS AND ROCKS AND THINGS

Along the walled lane adjacent to the paddock, then in front of the chapel, takes me down a well-trodden path, flourishing shrubbery to my left and gorse on the mountain side to my right as I head a few paces north to the Plantation. A wren bursts into song, warbling at full throttle and finishing with his familiar trill. Through a gate, avoiding the thickets and thorns of Nant Withy and walking instead into the avenues of trees that make up the Plantation. A blackcap, startlingly steel-grey and glossy black crown in the morning sun. An arresting sight. His song arresting too, jaunty, dancing phrases, rich music in the morning air. Chiffchaff sings monotonously, and yet it rings through the wood, presaging the shift of spring into summer. As I exit one part of the Plantation to enter another a small flock of siskin pass over, a faint whistling and twittering their accompaniment. In the wood I now enter, just through the conifer belt, a whitethroat sings. A goldcrest up in a conifer picks out insects from among the pine needles. I watch him for a while, intent on his feeding, then focus on the white throat of the whitethroat, singing from a sapling wych elm, stretched throat in soft, warm swell of song. Next is the sedge warbler, well overdue. From amongst the bramble-brakes his jumbled, scratchy song is heard; rasping and grating, trilling and whistling. Then out he flies.

Back down the main road and past Carreg Bach to the Observatory, the old farm house at Cristin, built for Lord Newborough in eighteen-seventy-four. The Observatory garden provides a splendid habitat both for residents and visitors to the island. Dunnock, wren, chiffchaff, blackbird, willow warbler and blackcap are immediately in evidence. High up in a conifer another goldcrest appears after about five minutes. Down below thickets of wild pear, cut back into tight hedges, provide excellent cover to ensure that the reed warblers are to be heard, even if less frequently seen. As I sit, back to the rising sun, a kestrel flies over from north to south.

Sitting in the garden of the Observatory presents a perfect panorama of the south-west corner of the island where the land runs into the sea, the seals find sanctuary, and the spring squill and thrift compete for the grassy spaces, obliterating them with pastel blue and pink, as the spring advances. I look to the rocky reefs, taste the clean, clear salt water, feel the ebb and flow of the place beneath, hear a bell pealing.

In prospecting flight a sparrow hawk glides in a circle over the mountain, beats its wings slowly and soars. I make my way across the Narrows and to the lighthouse.

A startled heron rises from its salt water stalking ground with heavy, flapping flight. I scour the west coast of the Narrows just south of Solfach Beach. My intended quarry the purple sandpiper. An elusive and unobtrusive bird, a small flock of which are reported as currently on Carreg yr Honwy, an island off Solfach Beach, described in eighteen-eighty-three as 'flat and about half an acre in area, a quarter of a mile out to sea and only visible at low tide.' So here I am overlooking the outermost point of the rocky headlands, opposite Carreg yr Honwy.

From some secret place, on reef or in gully, amongst rocks or seaweed grubbing, at once they rise. As one they flock, a small party of pilgrims, flight direct and fast. And yet there's something of wisps of smoke, blown by the wind back to Carreg yr Honwy. All of the elements enter them. They enter the elements.

On our first meeting, island-educated Connor, who has lived on Bardsey all fourteen years of his life, told me of the location of Merlin's cave on the mountain behind Carreg Bach. Next time I saw him he was completely preoccupied as he strutted by the cottage punching the air. Later that afternoon he passed by again in normal walking mode and I asked him what music he had been listening to earlier. His response was to play it to me. It was America's, 'A Horse with No Name.' A shared resonance shone through the lyrics.

> 'On the first part of the journey
> I was looking at all the life
>
> There were plants and birds and rocks and things
> There was sand and hills and rings.
>
> The first thing I met was a fly with a buzz
> And the sky with no clouds
>
> The heat was hot and the ground was dry
> But the air was full of sound.'

Two house martins in the early evening as I walk around the side of the cottage to fill my bucket with precious rainwater. The remainder of the day's journey was to comprise an illustrated talk on the Manx shearwater and a group outing with the Observatory warden and his two assistants. The Manx shearwaters' feet are set well back for swimming and tucking away for streamlined flight. A less advantageous consequence of this design feature is that they are completely inept on the ground. They can sit and they can walk, but the latter only after a stumbling fashion. And so they sit. And so they are caught. And so they are readily ringed. Meanwhile I try to re-live last Saturday night's solitary stargazing experience with the moon birds, as I hear whisperings of how old this bird is, how far this one has flown, how this one has not been ringed before. As there is no escape from the group, except into darkness, and with the

34

accompanying risk of falling off the cliffs into the Irish Sea, I remain on the periphery framing questions about the practice of ringing and whether any specific benefits accrue for the birds. Silence falls, apart from the strangulated cry of the shearwater, the occasional bubbling call of the whimbrel and the piping of the oystercatcher.

THE DEEP SKY AND THE DOMESTIC

Once more I wash my hair in rainwater. My hands, my feet and my et cetera. Ablutions completed and fast broken I saunter to the Abbey and adjacent graveyard. Set in stone, this I read:

Respect

> The remains of 20,000 saints
> Buried near this spot.
> Safe on this island
> Where each saint would be
> How wilt thou sail
> Upon life's stormy sea?

From one sacred place, to another; in a sacred place I saunter. Beyond the chapel and the Abbey ruins and above the gorse of gold and green a pair of peregrines fly swiftly through the mists of my mind, wing beats winnowing into graceful glide, soaring into the depths of the sky.

My island peregrinations continue with a move from the sublime into the domesticated quarters of the island. There is a beauty, if of a different sort, in the herd of Welsh black cattle, browsers and grazers, at home in the varied terrain, standing inscrutable as I watch. Black gold from the Welsh hills.

As I walk on by, the lambs, having drunk the milk of their dams' kindness, glory in their existence, exalting and intensifying through their play, the season that is spring. Then there's the billy goat, that proud son of Pan up at the farm; cloven hoofed, horned and bearded. Difficult to get away from the similarity to that diabolical depiction. Another harbinger of spring? Perhaps he taught the oystercatchers to play the pipes? After all the devil does have all the best tunes.

But who taught the blackbird to sing?

Bardsey Blackbird

Flirty tail dip and mellow flute
betrayed him once in bosky combe;
then, in heady ecstasy of afternoon's
torrid air, egg nestled in palm of hand
I let the heat stifle his cries of alarm.

Years on, he bathed in precious
water, in mother's garden shone
and taught me unknown things.

Now in twilight cool I walk,
from chimney stack and chapel pinking,
silhouette singing. Bardsey blackbird;
rich his repertoire ringing out,
and from fluting, mellow song

to chattering alarm
he returns me. And now I feel
flirty tail dip, sit, head cocked,
listen with him for the worm.

The remainder of that morning I spent in search of purple sandpipers.
And although I did not find any my search was not fruitless, for I found
instead so many manifestations of emergent spring:

*Lambs' tails, quivering in ecstasy; the thrill, the lift of squill and thrift
as I scramble over slippery rocks back into the springtime of childhood;
a trio of pipers, not purple, but the ubiquitous oyster catchers, engaged in a
mysterious ritual; in a circle, bills slightly open, heads bowed, joined by others,
piping resounding.*
   *Two pairs of wheatear, French grey of males' mating plumage,
crown and mantle, outstanding; one lone male still in search of a mate;
claims staked, oystercatchers and Atlantic grey seals, on the beach and in the water
at Solfach, inhabit their territory.*

The afternoon of that spring awakening found me once more on the mountain. Via the Observatory and the old school, I had made my way to Pen Cristin, the lesser celandine yellower still underfoot than last Tuesday, and looked out to sea from the south-east reaches of the island. So many swallows now, and the pair of ravens to keep me company. From here I travelled along a path which took me as far as it is safe to go on the east side of Mynydd Enlli. At the highest point I stood in the building wind, the ashlar limestone lighthouse, square-towered and red-and-white-banded to my right, the island of Carreg Ddu, and on the mainland Aberdaron, to my left. Giving myself over to the heights of the island I walk the spine of the Lord's Path and arrive at the northernmost part of Bardsey, buffeted in body but lifted in spirit by the big wind. Lying on the heather, bracken fronds unfurling, ravens roll, chough dance, gulls glide, the sea hisses. All enters me, I enter all.

ELUSIVE CUCKOO

We sail today at eleven a.m.

A saunter along the foot of the mountain to the chapel. The wrens, as ever, in full flood of song.

Back down to the Observatory. Linnets flying over, blackcap and chiffchaff the garden birds. Also a blackbird, a great favourite of the islanders. But the sparrows live on only as regrets. None since the sixties when a few shillings was the price on their grey or chestnut head. They wiped out the grain, the inhabitants wiped out the sparrows. All for a farmer's reward.

The house martins now such a sociable presence. These birds define the word gregarious. And as I walk again on the edge of the Withies the gorse, green and gold, gleams in the rain as the late morning light comes through.

The hens are scratching around the Observatory yard when I return to see if I can find the cuckoo which had been reported there earlier in the morning. In conversation with Connor I learn a little more about some of the domesticated animals that inhabit the island. On hens he is the expert. A bantam, grey mottled, goes by the name of Pepper. A splendidly glossy, black rock hen, as gracious and beautiful as Pertelote, is in fact called Chilli. There is already a pattern emerging in the names so it is no surprise when I am informed that a cuckoo-barred maran, layer of eggs of deep mahogany, only answers to the name of Cinnamon.

The cuckoo-barring on the exquisite plumage of this hen who lays the reddish-brown eggs is the closest I get to a cuckoo on this day of departure.

The elusive cuckoo, a marker for the mysteries of Bardsey. Heard but not seen on the day of arrival. Neither heard nor seen on the day of departure.

Sailed from Bardsey.

Up the lane to the car from the boat the blackthorn blossom is blooming from the buds of only a week ago. Bluebells nod their accompaniment in the light breeze. The gorse blazes; gleams on in the memory.

Spring Awakening

Spectral pilgrims of the night
become one flesh with the world;
reborn on Bardsey bathed in stars
blessed by combinations in colour
blessed by twenty thousand saints
confined in the deep and flying free,

world surrounded by blue-green water,
yellowish-orange and green-grey lichen,
stonechat dressed in orange-red breast,
brown-black swift over green-gold gorse,
reddish-brown eggs of cuckoo-barred maran,
glossed blue-black choughs, bracken unfurling,

willow copse welcoming, in territory unknown
I test for firm footholds; precious water purifying,
sacred air cleansing, I seek for grace flickering;
make my road by walking.

ULTIMA THULE

The first day of the trip was taken up with the rail journey from Worcester to Edinburgh, then on to Aberdeen. The second leg was unknown territory to me but I had, since about nineteen fifty-six, cherished the possibility of travelling the east coast rail route from Edinburgh to Aberdeen. It was worth the wait.

Anchored and counterbalanced by cantilevers, suspended over the Firth of Forth, viewing all things through suspension bridge strings, criss-cross cables of Queensferry Crossing and Forth Road Bridge, I am advanced into coastal cuttings over embankments allowing only glimpses of the sea. Walled with gorse, olive and gold, in the constraints of the cutting driving on; a narrow road to the deep north until wide waters open and the tranquil green sea, distant mountains, unfamiliar architecture of foothills, foment imagined mystery as I dream my way to Shetland, wind turbine blades, wheels of fortune, turning.

I glance back at the ordered arches, a perfect curve echoed in Tay bridge trajectory, before seascapes of sand, rock-stacks and the abundance of golden gorse deliver up ruins of red castle; and over sand dunes Lunan's sabre bay, sun's haze hanging in air, a dazzling reflection on the water, silhouetting the mountain range through which Phoebus will descend. Stonehaven, once Kilwhang after the sound of wind whistling, Dunnottar Castle, chapel ruins and burial ground; fingers of rock reaching out from the foundations of Dunnottar pointing the way to Shetland. Mist over the sea at the horizon; pink and grey sky, the violet hour approaching. Grey granite, rain on cobbles. Aberdeen in the present moment now passes to gannet and fulmar, my escorts ensuring a smooth sea crossing to Lerwick.

WHAT IS THE SOUND OF SHETLAND?

What is the sound of Shetland? he asked. And I listened, listened to stiff-winged maalie glide, hover, master the wind, wings raked, tail feathers fanned, all in silence; and I heard that on tiptoe alamootie dances over the waves to Mousa. I watched a raft of bonxie, tranquil in early evening on Spiggie Loch, and from Esha Ness saw a giant horse, silent as stone,

39

drinking salt water, and in that moment the wind was the voice of Shetland, the bite and bluster of the wind blowing around and through us as we walked the rough diamond of Ness of Hillswick. Becalmed in St Magnus Bay the granite stacks I learned to call the Drongs, sailing ships deaf to whistling winds, elemental sculptures carved by wind and water; wheelhouses at Jarlshof, once buried by wind-blown sand, revealed by violent storms, the primeval silence in the souterrain; tammie norie riding the wind alone, shrieking in silent joy, banking thrillingly as he shared his ecstasy on the headland at Hermaness.

RENEWAL

The high-pitched mewing drew my attention. On looking up I saw the silhouette of a hawk-like bird as it glided gracefully over Busta House Hotel. The straight and pointed projecting tail feathers announced the presence of an Arctic skua.

That day we drove from Brae to Toft. Ferried from Toft across Yell Sound to Ulsta on the island of Yell, then drove north from Ulsta to Gutcher. Ferried from Gutcher across Bluemull sound to Belmont on the island of Unst, then from Belmont drove almost the length of Unst to Boo Stacks.

On foot at last we entered a world of blanket bog and peaty pools, an open sward covering a deep carpet of peat. A treeless habitat of desolate grandeur. As we walked further along the shallow valley of the Burn of Winnaswarta Dale the group began to string out and it became increasingly difficult to feel in touch with the others. The habitat began to seem not only treeless but empty of life. All light filtered out by dust and mist, no sea to be seen, no crashing waves to be heard. The wind dropped and stillness began to surround me. Then for the first time I noticed the bonxies on the gentle slopes beyond. Heads above parapet they watched from the safe horizon of their nesting grounds. As I continued to walk the light grew steadily stronger and the bonxies more numerous, nowhere to hide in this unwooded place, the air utterly clear and silent now in a conjunction of landscape and legend.

The courtship display began with a bowing ceremony performed on the ground. In beatific beauty transformed from brute beasts these pirates and predators, perform a ritual of mutual protection. Bonxies, the divine, the celestial ones, prepossessing in chocolate-brown plumage, spotted and streaked with buff, mane of golden feathers on nape of muscular neck. And now in heavy but agile flight they soar together, wings half-raised in display, white wing flashes emblematic of angels. Barrel chests proudly puffed out, wings folded back, in their blissful serenity, burning bright, shedding light in their ecstasy, now soaring in circles over their nesting site.

'Kindness is the golden chain by which society is bound together.'

JOHANN WOLFGANG VON GOETHE

This uncharacteristic kindness mythologised in my bonxie story was, in fact, a notable feature of the Shetland Islands. The Busta House and Kveldsro House hotels proved hospitable throughout the stay. Fried bread on demand and milk made whole once more with the addition of cream to semi-skimmed. A kind island fellowship; the milk of human kindness. The return journey from Unst included a sighting of a group of otters living under the ferry terminal at Belmont. One was a strikingly big-built male with a fish; quite unperturbed by our presence as the captain kindly steered us round for a closer look.

Thule Charters provided a myth-making trip on board a catamaran. Around Bressay to Noss's giddying cliffs. Cliffs quarried for the stone that built Lerwick and salted away by the elements to steepling heights. Charles William Vane Tempest Stewart, the Marquis of Londonderry leased Noss from 1870 to 1900 for breeding Shetland ponies to replace child labour in his Durham coalmines. Is there any kindness in such a mix of cruelty and compassion I wonder?

THE NEW ORDER ON NOSS

A finely tuned network of cruciforms crowd the sky as gannets gather for a place in the gallery, blue sea beneath, guano and green algae on red-slashed sandstone rising above.

Juveniles hang out on Club Rock, bonxies, great black-backed gulls and hooded crows, opportunistic predators, wait patiently.

Kittiwakes confined to caves, and all auks, poor aliens now.

41

SHETLAND MUSEUM & ARCHIVES, HAY'S DOCK, LERWICK

What a place to learn about Shetland. So many artefacts. And music. A piece called *Spring*, a slow, lilting yet sad Shetland tune played on a gue, an early manifestation of a fiddle. Two strings of horsehair. After the gue, the fiddle. Tom Anderson, the Shetland master. Fiddler, composer, teacher, collector.

Other Shetland islanders from across the years peer out at the world. And, I imagine, at me. No selfies for them.

Much of the time I spent on Shetland looking out to sea. In hope of orca. But it was in this space, listening to a story, told by one of the receptionists, which recounted the day on which she and her children watched a pod of orcas in the dock, that my hopes were realised. So simple and yet so vivid was her retelling of the experience, through which she and her children had lived, that through this family I felt the majesty of the cetaceans.

Orca. Majestic and comely in proportion, whetted and oiled, fluted and chamfered, perfect symmetry held still in grace, in elegant ease moving and still: singing out a devotional ocean sea song.

Ocean sea. Something I have loved about the simple originality of combining those two words ever since Hilde Stroobants, an old friend from Leuven, sent me the novel of that name.

Oceano mare is a 1993 novel by the Italian writer Alessandro Baricco. Its narrative revolves around the lives of a group of people gathered at a remote seaside hotel. The novel won the Viareggio Prize. Reviewing the book for *The New York Times* Richard Bernstein wrote:

'*Ocean Sea* unfolds in its poetically elliptical way. Mr. Baricco is a literary cubist, a stylist who looks simultaneously at the several sides of things. He switches from one rhetorical mode to another, from a kind of symbolist poetry to grand adventure narrative to picaresque comedy.'

Tom Boncza-Tomaszewski of The Independent saw it as,

'A book about being, metaphysics juggled like the best trick of a wise old clown. This is a novel that at least suggests there's more to life than what any rationalist would tell you.'

Trowie Knowe. Night is their time. In the Knowe we find them. All shiny things are what they love. The fiddle pleases them. Trows will even teach one a tune. In the Knowe we find them and they are in the know. Of course they're imagined. But that doesn't mean they don't exist. They exist in that they are what we think we see in the cliff face, in water, in flames, in clouds. They may be troglodytes. They may be giants.

PARADISES

We look down on what appear to be two azure lagoons, one on either side of a slim isthmus of sand, the colour of clotted cream. The pull of the sea seems stronger than ever with the bonus of Eden Garden and other paradises lost which this isle of St Ninian's evokes. Dream-spaces, places of magic visions, lost worlds, rural idylls.

In tune with the Arctic terns returning, a walk takes us over the tombolo to St Ninian's Isle, where some of us search in the sand and paddle in the shallows. In the palm of this pilgrim's hand, a scallop shell. I look at its many grooved lines running from the outer rim to a meeting point at the base. Converging, or, if looking from the meeting point to the outer rim, diverging. The Scallop Shell is the emblem of St. James and has, over the years, been invested with symbolic significance. This symbolic significance relates to that aspect of the human condition commonly referred to as the spiritual. On this sacred, non-material level, our lives may be viewed as a metaphorical journey, unique to each individual and governed by the lessons that we learn and the people we become. To extend this metaphor, we do to some extent, walk similar or even the same roads, however, our highly subjective and private, inner pathways move through very different emotional landscapes and across terrain that cannot be fully known by others.

Arcadia

The site of the church on St Ninian's isle was a special place for burial before the advent of Christianity. Neolithic graves have been discovered there and to stand on the cliff top site of this pastoral paradise is particularly redolent of the conjunction of history, myth and landscape. The Poussin painting *Et in Arcadia ego* came to mind as I stood in this imagined Arcadia and putative home of Pan. The painting is of shepherds in an idyllic setting discovering and contemplating on the memorial inscription which translates as 'Even in Arcadia there am I'. The 'I' of the phrase refers to death, reminding us that death comes to us wherever we are.

The Elysian Fields

At the end of the earth on the banks of the Oceanus, an after-life for the righteous, imagined in this paradisiacal place where rock doves rise, Arctic terns dive and a lark climbs into the ether. I lie on my back among the asphodel and trumpeting narcissus, pillow of moss supporting my head as the lark's bel canto delivers me into the arms of my mother, lying as a child by her beloved 'luminous home of waters,' on bed of velvet grass, deeply stirred from joy, untouched by sorrow on the island of the blessed.

Treasure Island

I learn on the island that in 1958 a local school-boy discovered a treasure hoard in this treasure of a place. Treasured memories for he who found the treasure hoard. Treasured memories for me recalling this treasure of a place.

Utopia

Turnstone, starling, green sandpiper and little ringed plover picked over the tidal deposit of kelp together, as nine of us sat and picnicked as we picked over ideas with one another, a society in harmony, talking, and listening to the birds and to poetry and to the sea and the wind. To all the sounds of Shetland. The day before on the North Mavine peninsula we had climbed from Collafirth Hill up Ronas Hill. From this highest point on the Shetland archipelago we looked out on Yell Sound, the North Sea and the Atlantic Ocean. There was also an opportunity to look into a chambered cairn, the single cell burial chamber of a clan chief. Looking inwards, looking outwards, looking back on history.

Fjarå

Lerwick provided another taste of paradise in the ambrosia and nectar which are served in Fjarå. And as I dine like a deity looking out over the North Sea toward Norway the waves break silently on foundations of rock. Shetland mussels, garlic butter, shallots, a splash of Pinot Grigio, parsley and cream. Served with Fjarå bread. And the beer is from the Valhalla Brewery.

Across the road from Fjarå is a convenient Tesco selling lots of different stuff. What they cannot provide, however, is a portal to the distant past. But just beyond the Tesco store, on a small promontory reaching into Clickhimin Loch, lies Clickhimin Broch. There the portal may be found.

IN THE BROCH AT CLICKHIMIN

As I reached the Broch rain was falling heavily. Stair-rod rain and little sign of life. Mallard, coot, tufted duck and oystercatchers tucked into the shoreline. But another bird was also present. A recent arrival from Africa, having traversed tracts of sea to arrive in Shetland. And now too wet and tired to fly, this house martin sat on a gatepost as I walked into the Broch looking for some kind of shelter. This was provided in a hearth at the hub. And emanating outwards like the spokes of a wheel, stone piers under lintel arches and corbelled roofs. Disappointed to have lost sight of the poor, drenched bird, I began to explore the enclosures within the thick, drystone walls. This maze of passageways proved tricky to negotiate but eventually I gained sight once more of the world outside. The rain had stopped now and a small group of house martins flew past this window on the outside world, chattering excitedly and chasing insect prey. The presence of the other person did not surprise me. It was as if they had been standing there forever, welcoming and watching the birds, arriving to make their summer home in Shetland. I watched them watching the birds in fullness of flight, and as I watched the whole landscape appeared to lift itself out by the roots and hover in the air, as toward me clouds rolled, wave on wave, a tide of traffic driven by the moon, turning my thoughts to the open sea, from which I imagined this stranger had come. I wanted so much to say some words to this figure, but felt speechless in my confusion, when through the silence I heard a singing voice. It sang of the sea, it sang of the earth, through mind's greenstick fractures, into a space between the darkening of now, it sang of the sky. And into that skyspace I seemed to fly, to explore the world, from a hole perfectly engineered in night sky, which once I learned to call the moon.

And I trembled with fear as the voice that I heard was a voice that was mine, a voice that was frail and a voice that was strong, a voice with tone sweeter than strawberry wine. And the song that it sang was the song of the stranger, a song that possessed me and was sung now through me. It sang of the present, it sang of past danger, it sang of the dawnings that promised to be.

Kveldsro

Peace falls on Lerwick at the bothy,
origami gannet, wings folded flat,
lifts a gift from darkening waters,
a prelude to a familiar song;
another brother still singing out
after all these years.

Flirty tail dip and mellow flute
betrayed him once in bosky combe;
then, in heady ecstasy of afternoon's
torrid air, egg nested in palm of hand
I let the heat stifle his cries of alarm.

Now in twilight cool I walk,
from chimney stack
and kirk roof pinking,
a silhouette singing.
Lerwick blackbird,
rich his repertoire ringing out
with fluting, mellow song,
to chattering alarm returns me.

And now I feel flirty tail dip,
sit, head cocked,
listen with him for the worm.

BEYOND THE KNOWN WORLD

Bonxies bond on Hermaness; once spores, now florets of sphagnum moss,
whisper promises of peat. Gannets compose themselves, head, nape, body,
yellow and white, on white and red of guano and granite. As yet unseen a
storm petrel dances on the waves. This is still life, quality of light
colouring, shades and tints harmonising. To see as a painter, to find the
right word for a portion of spring squill and one bud of thrift, for a house
martin drenched at Clickhimin Broch; for the wind's teeth biting over rows

of graves on Knab End. Spring in the deep north and the mystery beyond and beneath. Winter currant and bluebells, triple rasp of hooded crow, pink granite, grey gneiss, sheer red cliffs. The known unknown. Ultima Thule.

RETURNING

Through the mist I watch the wake, taste the salt spray, listen to the waves' slam, feel the sea's acreage under and around. The sky on fire at sunset, the startling blue of the night sky, the slow sunrise. And the eiders in their hundreds, untroubled by troubled waters on the mudflats at Montrose.

SEVEN DAYS: BADIA DE POLLENCA, MALLORCA

'To lead life heedlessly, without reserve, entirely given over to the magic of the moment.'

STENDHAL

Mist clears and the morning dawns to reveal a sky of mother-of-pearl over the calm waters of the Badia de Pollenca. While this last breakfast is a lonely one, due to the later departure time of my fellow travellers, the view toward the still undiscovered bourn of Cap de Formentor reminds me of a reason to return to this part of Mallorca.

The coach journey to Palma is a dream, the big sky a wash of subtle tones; violet, lavender, lilac and turquoise paint the present moment of the morning and the ubiquitous spotted flycatcher flits and twirls through the air to take me back over the journey of the last seven days,

> 'Seven days, that were connected
> Just like I expected, they'd be coming on forth
> My beautiful comrades from the north.'

At the foot of the three hundred and sixty-five steps leading to the top of Calvi Hill the square offers shade. In the corner of the square the parish church of Our Lady of the Angels, Pollenca, offers much more as I step from shade into serene shade and am soothed by the sounds of muted music. This chiaroscuro world of chapel niches, dark corners and shadowed pools of escaping light gently illuminates saints and seraphim, the strongest lights in the darkness being the golden crown of Christ and the golden arrows of Saint Sebastian. Until, that is, I realise I am still wearing my sunglasses. I remove them to experience a florid fright of garish baroque churrigueresco. The daydream dissipates and I'm off the coach and into the departure hall of the Aeropuerto de Palma de Mallorca.

I check in and wander through the hallowed halls of Duty Free where only the Lavabos offer anything resembling refuge. And so I stand by the Hard Rock Cafe Shop trying to shut out 'Mama Weer All Crazee Now' while watching the swifts so close and the Tramuntana mountains now so distant, and await boarding time in the company of that man of mystery, *Nostromo*. I board the plane, 'Whatever You Want' still ringing out. And my answer is still the same. Some relief from Slade and Quo. Some more serenity. Some more reminders of the mysteries of the past seven days.

The Eleonora's falcon steadies me for take-off and I'm off again in search of this most elusive of promised birds. Was that indeed one, it was certainly the sleekest of falcons, as we entered Albufera for the very first and almost certainly not the last time. Named after Eleonora of Arborea, Queen and national heroine of Sardinia, who granted for the first time in history the protection of bird nests against illegal hunters in 1392. For some that explains the presence of so many Sardinian warblers. Legend has it that they are forever in search of her namesake, to give thanks to the falcon for benefitting, as they do, from Eleonora's enlightened approach to living and ruling. I console myself with the thought that perhaps the redness of their eyes accounts for *their* failure in finding this elusive falcon.

From myth to reality and a vivid recollection of the only hoopoe we saw, that's an *Upupa epops*, just before entering the National Reserve of Albufera. That was in amongst neglected suburban gardens where the bare or lightly vegetated ground on which to forage was perfectly suited to the bird's habitat requirements.

The rest of that day at Albufera offered many riches, including, almost immediately on entrance, the entrancing sight of a strung-out flight of glossy ibis; sickle-billed and long of legs. A little less co-operative, were the group of bee-eaters, perhaps looking for a place to colonise along the sandy canal bank, judging by their restless back-and-forth behaviour and discreet dropping down behind the reeds.

Walking this world of marshes and dunes, vegetation of reed and sedge, and white poplar, elm and tamarisk trees, we were stopped in our tracks by a bird that sounded like a nightingale. And to make us more certain it did not appear. But oh, the ever-reliable inconsistency when later in the week this assumption of its shyness was turned on its head.

To be able to list so nonchalantly the hoopoe, glossy ibis and bee-eater served to demonstrate for us the plethora of new birds. But for me the special bird of this first full day on Mallorca had to be the black-winged stilt. I found it to be as preposterously delicate and unusually beautiful as I had always imagined. Standing shakily and sitting on the nest clumsily, but in flight not far removed from a seraphim, the highest order of the celestial hierarchy, aflame with light, ardour, and purity.

So many of these birds were seen from the Aguait des Colombars Hide, a mirador as revelatory, if not quite so charged with poetry, as the towers of William Butler Yeats or Rainer Maria Rilke. And although there was another poetic omission in that our tower was not inhabited by *The Lady of Shalott* we did have the lady from Amsterdam who talked a lot. Very helpful she was too in drawing our attention to the common pochard and the little grebe. And then the osprey, as patient and still as Simeon Stylites on his pillar.

After a gap of ten years it's wonderful to be flying again. Such new-found freedom in these early days of living on the wing once more. No horizon to limit my horizons. A flight so smooth and free of turbulence I can close my eyes and relax. As if becalmed in the air we are once again in mountains and in vales.

Was that an Eleonora's falcon out of my side of the coach that served as a moving mirador, commanding an extensive outlook on the return from lake Cuber? Too indolent, following the serenity of a saunter in a sun-soaked basin in the Tramuntana Mountains, to bother Pam and Chris with the possibility. I recall it was in the purlieus of Puerto Pollenca. coasting and diving next to an olive grove. But what I remember most vividly is now a kind of splendid uncertainty; of not quite properly experiencing the bird. We know when we really know it, not with a glimpse, but with all of our discerning senses in operation.

'Solitary in the field, senses sharpened. To sit and wait brings one into harmony with the pulse of the day.'

JOHN BUSBY

Framed by the welcome of a nightingale, and the unique valedictions in the form of a snake swimming and making waves, we ambled around lake Cuber, griffon and black vultures soaring over the peaks of the Tramuntanas. And that really did look like a Dartford warbler just before our return journey. However, we were informed later, by a helpful and amusingly competitive birding couple, that this would be a subalpine warbler. Over the grasslands surrounding Albufereta a zigzag flight with zitting calls, a bird reminiscent of a parachuting meadow pipit, was pointed out to us as a zitting cisticola. The warbler of the zit and cist, now that's an easy one to recall. At this point Chris remembered to ask about the yellow-legged gulls and it was confirmed that these indeed were the gulls on lake Cuber.

The serenity that characterised the walk around lake Cuber is reawakened as we fly on a cushion of billowing clouds over the Mediterranean. My reverie is sustained by those magical mountains and the little world they contained. And now those lake Cuber chaffinches appear once more, such coruscatingly pristine plumage prompting the return of a vision of the gleaming promise of yet another possibility. A pilgrimage to the Santuari de Lluc. Another reason to return?

As the pilot relays a message about the perfect view of Paris beneath us I, in my reveries, am introduced by my comrades from the north to the dark brown peapods of the carob trees. A chocolate substitute they inform me. The Boquer Valley where this occurred was altogether a place of surprises. The experience was crowded with feelings that anything could happen on a walk at first along narrow paths walled in by barren rock, through scrub and pine trees, then flanked by precipitous mountains on either side, one threatening to fall away and the other leaning over as if about to collapse in folds and block our way. Then the surprise of the open sea. Rising like a vision out of the barren land. We had come through. And with us the growing knowledge that the red-eyed Sardinian warbler must be the commonest bird in these parts.

But surprises weren't confined to the Boquer Valley. After our descent from Puig di Maria a bird on the wire that turned out to be a budgerigar. And a lovely moment early on just outside the hotel when both Pam and I fell for an unusually white gull with a beady eye and a pretty face. The red lip-sticked bill was diagnostic, as was the black of the wing tips in flight. This Audouin's gull, a spring and summer visitor to Mallorca, became a favourite. And turning to a different sort of surprise for we three northerners, if I dare claim to share in that honourable title after spending most of my life in Worcester, to be served in a restaurant by a lass from Ashington and then be hailed from a table next to us by a couple from Embleton – now that is really something in downtown Port de Pollenca.

A bus from the Port de Pollenca to Pollenca, then a walk from the suburbs of Pollenca across the Pont Roma into the purlieus of Ternelles – a market garden of adobe haciendas and the wealth of nations' properties. Chris flashes his credentials and before we know it some creatures with a talent for singing like croaking, laughing birds – male marsh frogs in fact, vocal sacs inflated, attempting to attract females – are accompanying us along the path by the Torrent de Ternelles, through woods and parkland to the Castell del Rei – another Tennysonian moment when 'The splendour falls on castle walls'; a castle growing out of the living mountain.

This was a unique walk requiring permission to walk in what was presumably once a privileged preserve for royal hunting. The sounds and sights included, though not for me, a red male Balearic crossbill that made me as green with envy as the female of the species (which I also missed – this one at my own private Gola). Yes, I know. Another reason to return.

For two early morning stints (not the little waders!) I was on my own in my own Gola. Empty streets, apart from a couple of dog walkers and joggers, and swifts sweeping over the rooftops.

On the first morning the insects had been low on the water when I arrived and it wasn't long before the swifts were swooping amongst them. Swallows and house martins soon followed and during this clean-up operation three swallows settled down obligingly in an alder. They had a great view of the insects and I of them. Male stonechats too made themselves visible for anyone who cared to admire their handsome figures. Heads so black it's difficult to see their eyes, while the white sides to the neck and the russet/orange breast left no question about their readiness for breeding.

The second morning was marked by three Audouin's gulls holding me up for a moment as they crossed the zebra crossing. What a marvellous image. Just one bird short of the Beatles. Not the numbers of hirundine and swifts this morning. They were all much higher up. But some very different sounds and sights greeted me on this visit. A chiffchaff calling its onomatopoeic call, a wheezing greenfinch and then a linnet settling on a pine tree. With the sparrow family on the boardwalk under the trees and a moorhen and mallards feeding, this began to feel like a quintessential English country scene. Until the intervention of a Sardinian warbler's rasping, rattling, chatter disabused me of this fanciful Anglocentric notion.

Two spotted flycatchers feeding in unison and the jingling, tinkling sound of serin relocated me in Mallorca. Then as I left it was the turn of two herons, both alike in dignity, to take the stage to perform what could have been a threat or a courtship display. Buenos Dais said a passing stranger. I paused, returned the greeting then left for breakfast and the opportunity to rehearse my newly acquired facility with the Spanish lingo.

The demonstration of my new found language skills didn't go quite as planned because of some forgetful slippage which took me from Spain to Italy and from morning to evening. Buona Sera says I to two puzzled looking waitresses as I swan into Sis Pins, our hotel for the week. Then to top that I was congratulated by two fellow visitors who I then proceeded to give the benefit of my knowledge of Spanish. Fortunately for all three of us one of the waitresses intervened to explain the error of my ways.

This breakfast memory reminds me of another great surprise, that being one of the best ever home-made spag bols in living memory. That was in a garden restaurant in Port de Pollenca to celebrate Chris's birthday. The best beer of the holiday as well as it happens, brewed up the road in the never-to-be-forgotten Medieval walled town of Alcudia. And what sort of restaurant? Why, vegetarian, of course.

At Can Callerassa Pam spoke of nightingales with a couple, and we learned to turn on its head the assumption that nightingales are rarely seen. At that very moment I had turned my head towards what was the most confident possible sighting of the elusive one. A large swift. Slender, with long, narrow wings. Hunting hobby-like for insects. But would there really be only one? And even if it was why did no one else mention it?

Our second visit to Albufereta was useful for sorting out the serins and endeavouring to ascertain the differences between ringed plover, little ringed plover and Kentish plover. The last mentioned only familiar from my Collins Pocket Guide to British Birds or else my Observer's Book of Birds, both 1959.

Another possible Eleonora's falcon in the afternoon at Albufera? Now this seemed like it could be the beginnings of many more. But since that didn't happen I have grown less and less certain. And with three pairs of eyes too we covered a fair area of the reed-beds. The black crowned night heron, a bulkier bird than the purple, and those give-away long, thin and very sparse crest feathers that Chris appeared to envy so much, was some considerable consolation. But the best birding moment of this day for me was when the three of us had a perfect sighting of a marsh harrier, drifting low and circling and quartering the marshes and reeds with occasional but powerful beats of the wings. On the coach on the day of departure I had imagined that an Eleonora's had to be waiting somewhere along the long road home. Somewhere. Maybe it still is? Yet another reason to return.

Gia mi fur dolci invite a empir le carte il uoghiameni.
'These pleasant places were once, for me, a sweet invitation to write.'

ARIOSTO

HEBRIDEAN HOLY DAYS

'The untold want by life and land ne'er granted,
Now, Voyager, sail thou forth, to seek and find.'

WALT WHITMAN

OBAN – MULL

Lyndon delivers us safely to Oban, into the hands of Chris the skipper. A swift embarkation and we are on our way to the Sound of Mull. Loch Sunart, a sea loch on the south side of the Ardnamurchan peninsula takes us to our first mooring at Loch na Droma Buidhe, or Loch Drambuie as Stevie the cook refers to it. I rather enjoy Stevie's accompanying legend of Bonnie Prince Charlie hiding in amongst the heather and coming up with the concept of heather honey whisky liqueur and am disappointed to find that the origins of Drambuie have only ever been traced to a secret recipe, created for Bonnie Prince Charlie in the eighteenth century by his Royal Apothecary.

The cloud banks forming a low curtain on the Ardnamurchan peninsula promise some imminent magic. And this is not slow in coming when we retire to the sights of red deer and the sound of a cuckoo calling, and wake to see, at seven o'clock in the morning, three otters slipping sleekly through the water.

MULL – CANNA – BARRA

At eight in the morning we depart for Canna, sailing past Muck, Eigg and Rum, in the company of a harbour porpoise, to disembark and experience the island of Canna, the westernmost of the small isles archipelago in the Inner Hebrides.

Canna, in what turns out to be searing heat when set next to my expectations of Scottish weather, provides a wonderful opportunity to see, among others, a colony of common gulls, a handsome wheatear and a white-tailed eagle. But, on hearing the caressing hush of a mellifluence thrilling and soothing, and seeing the soft swell of the stretched throat, strained with song devotional, it's the whitethroat that lingers on.

Round the other side of Canna to experience natural selection in action. Puffins wheeling, flotillas of guillemot and razorbill, kittiwakes calling their eponymous cry. And, witness to 'Nature, red in tooth and claw' in the midst of such profusion of life, the death of what we thought was a kittiwake, drowned by a great skua, perhaps better known as a bonxie. On closer inspection of the photographic evidence, so much creation and chaos had disguised the fact that the victim was a herring gull, rather than a kittiwake. Leaving the Isles of Skye and Canna in our wake, we head for Barra. In the open waters from Canna to Barra, some of the true ocean birds, gannet, Manx shearwater and fulmar accompany us. Common dolphin briefly join us too. And a basking shark, beautiful in its slow gliding, barely perceptible movement, darkly yet harmlessly just under the surface. Something of an eating machine this primeval fish.

Grey seals assemble to watch us inquiringly as we moor north-east of Barra.

BARRA – THE MONACHS

To the Monachs. Started on our way during breakfast. A lighthouse once again shows us the way. This one on Shillay. The Monach Lighthouse was built by Thomas and David Stevenson. The latter, Robert Louis Stevenson's father. The tender to the bay near the lighthouse allowed us to explore these machair covered and treeless islands, home to Arctic and little terns, rock and meadow pipits.

Braced for the swell, sea underfoot, now I'm walking on water.

It felt to me as if there was the beginning of a growing swell as we had approached the Monachs but Chris the skipper informed me that throughout the voyage the sea state never became worse than Slight or Moderate. Moored at the Monachs. A hen harrier heralds the morning, then, along with a house martin, we are heading for St Kilda.

THE MONACHS – ST KILDA

We had travelled from the Sea of the Hebrides through the Sound of Barra and into the Atlantic Ocean. Like two teeth in the jaw of a mountain range, a peak and a stac rose in front of us from under the vastness of an otherwise seemingly empty ocean. This was St Kilda. In the middle of the Atlantic Ocean. But was Nick's idea going to work? The concoction he had brought along to attract storm petrels felt like, well, a drop in the ocean. 'O ye of little faith,' rang in my ears as the fulmar began to arrive and to feed on the spreading oil slick of Rice Krispies. Nick had told me of the scent, the slick and the food as we travelled from Worcester to Fernhill Heath in his car on the first stage of our Hebridean journey, and had then repeated the ingredients to others as we travelled Saturday through Monday over land and sea. And now more tubenoses were definitely on their way. Next to arrive were the storm petrels.

All of us were watching in some delight over the port bow when out popped Captain Chris to ask what the little black birds were on the starboard side. Binoculars were raised and re-directed. Even more storm petrels where the split slick had spread itself. As we drank it all in what should fly over the boat, then land on the water to give us an even better view? Nothing but a pomarine skua. What a day. What a trip. And it was not even half way through.

White-beaked dolphins were briefly bow-riding before we moored up in Village Bay. Feet on dry land once more for my first taste of Kilda. A walk up through An Lag Bho'n Tuath, a corrie at the head of a valley dominated by four large drystone enclosures and some curious mounds on the glacially formed moraine of various sized boulders and pebbles. Boat shaped burial cairns? Old cleits? Viking graves? To The Gap to lie on Kilda soil and look in the midst of mystery over the edge of the world. Where am I? Somewhere in the Atlantic Ocean.

'Snowy owl' cries Nick as we walk along Mullach Sgar, strung out along this Old Way, toward Lover's Stone. At first disbelief then silence and awe as over our heads flew the Great White Wonder. Golden-yellow eyes and feathered feet clearly visible as we stood transfixed. Then the 'Wows' filled the empty air as Nick, Vanessa, Sheila, Jane and I gave voice to our feelings.

This is Hirta, one of the group of remote islands and sea stacs in the North Atlantic, that make up St Kilda. One hundred miles off the west coast of Scotland. It consists of dolerite, microdiorite, microgranite and blocks of ultrabasic rock, eucrite and gabbro. But these rocks are not the only things that lie at the root of its mystery. There is also the little world of wonder of carnivorous plants such as sundew and butterwort, the deep blue milkwort, believed to increase the milk yield of cows and nursing mothers, and now a great favourite of mine, the not uncommon but to me quite beautiful little yellow flower, which Vanessa informs me is tormentil. Add in the drumming of snipe, and the success of our expedition in our patient search for the St Kilda wren, to understand the magic properties of this place. Then sit by the Mistress Stone and look over to Dun where puffins and fulmar proliferate and the bonxies, together with the more streamlined version of a skua, the Arctic skua, employ their different feeding strategies.

Having now seen a bonxie dispatch a herring gull I am less inclined to mythologise the great skua as I did on Shetland. But, as Browning reminds us, these creatures are not acting without compunction. They have no guilt or moral scruple that prevents them doing something that certainly some humans would regard as immoral or unethical.

'No creatures made so mean,
But that some way, it boasts, could we investigate,
Its momentary task, gets glory all its own,
Tastes triumph in the world, pre-eminent, alone.'

ROBERT BROWNING

HIRTA – BORERAY – HARRIS

Something in the region of sixty-thousand pairs of gannets are on Boreray and the surrounding stacs. While we watch the spectacle of countless numbers of them plunge-diving into shoals of fish, minke whales allow us to share the water with them. And it's difficult to draw ourselves away from St Kilda with these irresistible visions of birds and cetaceans.

As we head for The Sound of Harris 'the petrel and the porpoise' are 'on the vast waters' but the sea is glassy and the petrels' white rump, slightly hooked bill, and tubular nostrils are clearly visible.

There's another side to these diminutive storm petrels, or alamooties, to which I am also attracted. That is their place in the culture of the sea. Mother Carey is a supernatural figure personifying the cruel and threatening sea in the imagination of sailors of the eighteenth and nineteenth centuries. Her 'chickens' were the storm petrels, mythologised by sailors to be the souls of dead seamen. As Mother Carey seems likely to be derived from the Latin, Mater cara, precious mother, and perhaps the Virgin Mary, it could be that the birds were seen as good or bad omens. The protectors presaging a storm or harbingers of death?

The Sound of Harris and a walk from Leverburgh to Loch Rodel. Cuckoo heard calling, then so clearly seen. Golden eagle at a distance. Twite and a whooper swan. Dwarf willow growing from a wall.

HARRIS – THE SHIANTS

Breakfast on the move. Now a favourite meal of mine. 'A cold collation' as Melanie clepes it. 'Continental in style.' I dine on Weetabix followed by a maple and pecan plait.

On to the Shiants. And it really is the serene dream which Adam Nicolson promised in *The Seabird's Cry*.

Stonechat, such a neat little bird, sits uncharacteristically calmly. No tail flicking, no harsh alarm call, but a rapid warbling song reminiscent of a dunnock or a whitethroat. Around him, English stonecrop, tormentil, dwarf willow and cotton grass. Serenity and an empty page.

A change in mood as hearing the undertow my heart heaves and I watch over the edge of a bay and directly into a cliff face where a pair of fulmar, together in their mystery, inhabit a world we cannot really know. I

57

watch the response of this tranquil pair on the arrival of a third bird. All three hold their ground, but the pair raise their open bills and cackle raucously to the air as the intruder turns his back, then as the pair quieten down the third calls loudly to an imagined mate. The pair persevere in their shared posturing and the third bird flies off. This happens three times, until, at the end of the third display the two settle down together once more and the third bird does not return. Referring to his observations of fulmar in *The Seabird's Cry*, Adam Nicolson reflects as follows.

'Sometimes looking at the fulmar's gaping, mouth-opening, mutually frenzied, head-bobbing, nibbling, shout-laughing, which can begin calmly enough but then builds to a tumultuous, guffawing, totalising climax, I have thought that only in the ecstatic moments of life can we come near to knowing the reality of a bird's mind.'

THE SHIANTS – HARRIS

At four-thirty we sail into Loch Tarbert to moor for the evening.

HARRIS – SOAY

A pair of red-throated divers. Then otters again. Two of them playing, as a cuckoo called. On their backs, in their element, rolling and tumbling. Then the female disappeared. And the big dog of a male, fish grasped to his belly, did the classic otter munching. Then he dived, climbed up the bank and ran over the grassy knoll, as though to give me more room for writing.

From Loch Tarbert we head down to the West Coast of Skye. The uncracked mirror of the glassy sea gives no glimpse of future or past. In all directions it stretches and spreads, surrounding the insignificant Elizabeth G., the immense waters lying in eloquent silence of mute greatness, their indifference reassuring rather than threatening, in that present moment, that moment of being.

Then the kittiwakes. The colony on Skye and a special event as porpoise and dolphin appear.

West Coast Spectacle

Feel the silence descend
as we all apprehend
porpoise gently tearing
the surface of the sea.

Then we delight in dolphin dining,
our amuse-bouche, a minke whale.

THE AFTER-DINNER BAIT BALL

In a welter of black and white a concatenation of porpoise, dolphin, gulls, gannets and skuas crank up ostinatos of boiling water as the wistful wailing of kittiwakes pursued by those graceful and buoyant bosun birds, the Arctic skuas, resonates over the open waters; dolphins dawdle, gannets split the surface with the splashes of flying clippers, origami wings folded flat, and minke whales make an appearance before a storm petrel flies in to pick up the scraps.

Soay island but not the one comprising part of St Kilda. This one is just off the south-west coast of Skye. This, however, is yet another island of great character, and one to which the tender delivers us. The basking shark fishing station was established here by Gavin Maxwell. Between 1945 and 1948 the huge carcasses were pulled out of the water, the livers rendered for oil, the rest sold for fertilizer, aphrodisiacs or food.

A cuckoo calls over this sparsely inhabited island where woods of birch, rowan and oak, together with rampant bracken, and conifers and rhododendrons from the abandoned gardens, determine the unusual habitat.

No evening stars to sing us to rest after another thrilling day. Unless, of course, one counts the newly formed quartet of Jane, Sheila, Lyndon and myself serenading the night with *In Dreams*, *Things* and *24 Hours from Tulsa*.

A great northern diver with a fish, and the cuckoo calling, close the day.

SOAY – HYSKEIR – EIGG

The morning begins with the sighting of a common seal and cuckoos audible and visible, before we sail around Soay and toward Hyskeir, breaking our fast (which fast is that?) on the move.

Eight-thirty a.m. Dolphin alert. For the lucky few, some bow-riding. And then the Arctic terns' alarm cries as they crowd the sky and the goblin chuckles of the great black-backed gulls tell me wherever I am, I am in the here and now. This is Hyskeir. Existential island. Basalt stacks and knotted wrack give a sense of a bleak but not barren island. A plateau of rock. It is, essentially, a birds' island. But it belongs to the flowers too. English stonecrop, flag iris, and when we invaded its privacy, especially the yellow blaze of bird's foot trefoil.

Caves for the majority. A partial ascent for two. Seven ravens cross our path in low and heavy flight as we walk up toward Sgurr of Eigg, the Nose of Sgurr sniffing us out. The highest hill on Eigg, formed as the result of one of the last eruptions of a volcano. The lava cooled to form basalt columns as on Hyskeir. After waiting in vain for what Shane MacGowan of The Pogues referred to as, 'the lonesome corncrake's cry of sorrow and delight' we walk a little further and the air is filled with birds. Book-ended by a trio of willow warblers and rock doves, tree pipit, redpoll and a flock of sulphur-yellow siskin, stamp themselves indelibly on my memory.

Moored at Eigg for the evening.

EIGG – MULL

An otter-disrupted breakfast provides all fellow-travellers with views of these delightful creatures.

Then another guide in the form of a lighthouse. We make our way toward Rubha nan Gall lighthouse, north of Tobermory on the Isle of Mull. The name means 'Stranger's Point' in Scottish Gaelic. Courtesy of Captain Chris some perfect views of white-tailed eagles and one golden eagle with an eaglet. Crag clasping, or perched on dead trees, and sometimes tricky for some of us to see. Such a big bird to miss so I was certainly appreciative of Margaret's capacity for ornithological navigation when she steered me faultlessly to the bird. On another occasion, as everyone else watched one bird, Jane managed to find her eagle-eyes to spot an alternative eagle.

Although not literally, Lismore and Lismore Lighthouse had lighted the way. Late afternoon we disembark to walk along a sea loch, Loch Spelve. We hear the sound from some distance away but it is a while before the great spotted woodpecker draws our attention to the young she is feeding in a telegraph pole. These and the young wood warbler point the way to the birth of the early evening, and another day to follow. The last of this glorious trip, and our time to journey home.

Moored in Loch Spelve.

Stevie sings a fine goodbye with *The Green Fields of France* and *The Wild Mountain Thyme*.

MULL – OBAN

This is very strange. We actually have a cold morning.

'When thou seest an Eagle, thou seest a portion of Genius; lift up thy head!'

WILLIAM BLAKE

At this point Nick's list totalled ninety-eight birds. As we step onto the pavement in Oban, Nick follows Blake's advice and spots something else. A jackdaw makes ninety-nine. Swiftly followed by a swift to make one hundred.

**'Old men ought to be explorers
Here or there does not matter
We must be still and still moving
Into another intensity
For a further union, a deeper communion
Through the dark cold and the empty desolation,
The wave cry, the wind cry, the vast waters
Of the petrel and the porpoise.'**

TS ELIOT

CARPE DIEM

'Every day there's one less day to seize.'

SALMAN RUSHDIE

St MARY'S

'Morning has broken, like the first morning,
Blackbird has spoken, like the first bird.'

ELEANOR FARJEON

It was, however, the true notes of the song thrushes which broke the silence of this first day on the mountain tops of the lost land of Lyonesse, more familiarly known as the Isles of Scilly.

The southern coast of St Mary's Island and the nature trail a little further inland offered up granite forms sculpted by sea and wind, and a wide range of habitats, from the seashore to reed beds, and through the airport via scrubland and gorse bushes, to Porth Hellick Pool, swallows swooping around our feet and pristine house martins omnipresent.

Exploration of the island continued through late morning and the afternoon, the beaches of Porthmellon and Porthloo revealing the varying characteristics of St Mary's. Further north to tranquil Toll's Porth the beach proved more idyllic while Bant's Carn Burial Chamber and the ancient village of Halangy Down provided evidence of the age of the island. This evidence is of an extensive and permanent settlement from around 2500 BC. A place which rang with resonances of a time when the sea level was lower and much of the Isles of Scilly formed a single landmass.

Along the north east coast haven that was Watermill Cove and Pelistry Bay, then a pause at Carn Vean tea garden where our thirsts are slaked with ice cream and we are nourished with the sight of a solitary swift.

That evening provided two more sources of nourishment. First of all in the form of an early evening meal in 'On the Quay.' Then a voyage to the uninhabited isle of Annet.

ANNET

'It is a beauteous evening, calm and free,
The holy time is quiet as a Nun
Breathless with adoration.'

WILLIAM WORDSWORTH

Wordsworth penned the perfect words for how our two-hour evening voyage began. At eight o'clock we sailed over a sea, which was somewhere between slight and moderate, into a stunning sunset. The fast, direct flight of gannets, bright white in the limpid light of the slowly setting sun, their black wing tips and yellow-buff head and neck so clear to see. These gannets proved to be the first birds to allow us to share the ocean with them. Another true ocean-going bird, the fulmar, with its characteristic stiff-winged flight also put in an early appearance and sooner than we might have expected the Manx shearwater started to arrive and began rafting up in readiness for their evening trip onto the safe nesting haven that is Annet. Alongside these properly mysterious birds were some remarkably close–up views of great northern diver riding the ocean swell.

This first taste of the open Atlantic brought with it a sense of the power of the sea around the Isles of Scilly. Lying just north-west of St Agnes, and with its treacherous looking jagged Haycocks as its northern-most point, Annet may be a perfect sanctuary for sea-birds but has been the cause of death for many sailors. The setting sun revealed it at its most bleak yet beautifully dramatic.

Many people commented on the brilliance of the moon that night, and as we turned to return to St Mary's the waxing crescent moon was moving imperceptibly toward its first quarter. According to the Greek Philosopher Aristotle and the Roman historian Pliny the Elder, human minds were influenced by the pull of the moon in the same way as are the tides. Is there any credence, I wondered, in the idea that, after recharging under the new moon, the waxing moon may be seen to represent the opportunity for intentions, hopes, and wishes to be planted. It was after midnight when I returned to Waverley, my temporary residence throughout this trip. 'Play me a song, Mr. Wolfman Jack.' I request Tom Waits', 'Anywhere I lay my head, that's my home,' in basso profundo deep and richly dark under a skyful of stars and promises.

The following day was a relaxing one in which we further familiarised ourselves with St Mary's Island. Wrens provided the sound-track for a heath-land walk along the coastal path from Hugh Town to Old Town, but when we arrived at St Mary's Old Church graveyard it was 'the wise thrush' who won us over.

In the middle of the island adjacent to the aptly named Holy Vale, Carreg Dhu Gardens, a magnificently neglected space, provided tranquillity among the succulent aloes and yuccas and ostentatious trumpet trees. Cordylines from Australia and spruce from Prussia, along with aloes and stately palms, define this habitat, a unique combination of the natural and the managed. Carreg Dhu or Black Rock was once quarried but has been converted into a garden, part wild, part cultivated, by volunteers from the local community.

The rich jaunty warble of the blackcap, well concealed until revealed by watchful ears and listening eyes, serenaded us in these serene surroundings.

TRESCO

'That's the wise thrush; he sings each song twice over,
Lest you should think he never could recapture
The first fine careless rapture!'

ROBERT BROWNING

Awoken by the competing song thrushes of St. Mary's Island. An early morning walk to the Garrison to look out over the isles of St Agnes and Annet. Distance and daylight have reduced the palpable hazard of the Haycocks; what had felt threatening at night, was now, in the stillness of the morning, a reassuring picture of rocks glistening silver under the soft sunlight. Looking out over the ocean the splashes of the plummeting gannets break the silence along with an intermittent chorus of lesser black-backed gulls. Together with the stonechats, starlings, house sparrows and numerous song thrushes seen on our walk to the quay for a trip to Tresco, this diversity of species in a small area proved characteristic of the Isles of Scilly.

Although famous for the Abbey gardens, golden pheasant and red squirrel we decided to explore the natural habitats of Tresco before enjoying the more accessible pleasures of the island.

Oliver Cromwell, Lord Protector of England has a surprising

prominence on Tresco. Symbolically built out of stone from the demolished King Charles' Castle, Cromwell's Castle is a fortification that survived from the Interregnum, the period between the execution of Charles I in 1649 and the Restoration of Charles II in 1660. A startling remnant of republicanism this round tower stands on a promontory guarding the anchorage between Bryher and Tresco. Strategically significant, this was one of the main routes of entry to the heart of the Isles of Scilly and the deep-water approach to New Grimsby Harbour.

As it turned out we spent so much time enjoying the history and the varied habitats of the island there was insufficient time to visit the sub-tropical garden carved from bare moorland. Instead we took a clockwise route around the coastal paths with views over the water to Bryher, St Martin's and St Mary's. As well as the seascape there was heath-land inhabited by stonechats, arable land and areas of woodlands and wetlands.

The wrinkled sea, the roaring waters, the blasted heath and the struggling light. Hunched buzzard in lichen-lined tree hides from what feels like the returning winter. A carrion crow croaks in the cold air. Shadows are cast in the confusion of an osier's strong-limbed, yet supple branches. An immense large-leaved lime, gnarled and twisted and repeatedly split and bifurcated so that it stands as at least six trees in one. A peregrine soars into the surprise of a blue sky, as the theatre of my imagination is fired up with echoes from an earlier time. Is this the Tresco believed by some to be the last resting place of Arthur of the Britons? Segged brogues strike parquet floor and I'm in the presence of that man once more. Not only did he relish the recitation of Tennyson's re-telling of *Morte d'Arthur*, this was also among the gems that Basher Grey passed on to many of those who were in hearing distance of its occasional performance. Passed on, not through a reading and accompanying explication of the text; rather, it seems in retrospect, through a process of unconscious assimilation; of osmosis. Of King Arthur. Of Lyonesse. Of Bedivere. Of 'a broken chancel with a broken cross.'

SAMSON, BRYHER & ISLANDS BETWEEN

Hugh Town to Samson
Samson to Green Island
Green to Puffin Island
Puffin to Great Rag Ledge
Great Rag to Paper Ledge
Paper to Conger Ledge
Conger to Yellow Ledge
Yellow to Broad Ledge
Broad to Diamond Ledge
Diamond to Lizard Point
Lizard to Hedge Rock Ledge
Hedge Rock Ledge to Hedge Rock
Hedge Rock to Tean
Tean to St Helen's
St Helen's to Round Island
Round Island to Men-a-vaur
Men-a-vaur to Golden Ball
Golden Ball to Tresco
Tresco to Bryher

From Hugh Town, the largest town on the largest island of the archipelago, we head at first towards a large but uninhabited island going by the name of Samson. Not, as I at first imagined, named after the Old Testament Samson who was depilated by Delilah. Rather it was St Samson of Dol, a Christian religious figure born in the fifth century in southern Wales and who visited the Isles of Scilly. Stopping short of Samson we cruise slowly up the east coast of Green Island and over a sandbank to Puffin Island. A circuit of Puffin Island provides no sign of puffin but does take us along Great Rag Ledge and within sight of Tresco. Two kittiwakes roost on a rocky outcrop, submitting to the sea in perfect balance. Rounding the southern extremes of Tresco is a thrilling journey alongside more ledges of rock – Paper, Conger, Yellow, and Broad. Diamond Ledge, due north to Lizard Point, with sightings of well camouflaged turnstone. The dunlin, sanderling and ringed plover are a little easier to see. Then through the Scylla and Charybdis of Hedge Rock Ledge and Hedge Rock, to the Island of Tean. The remains of a chapel and chambered cairns is a reminder of a time in which this small isle was once inhabited. Sharing the ocean with guillemots and razorbills and the occasional fulmar sweeping low over the water, we sail up the west coast to St Helen's and on to Round Island then tight and snug through the straits of Men-a-vaur. The next phase of our voyage is Golden Ball to the Northern tip of Tresco with great views of Cromwell's Castle and the remains of Charles's Castle. Into New Grimsby Quay for some to disembark. Others of us cross the New Grimsby Harbour to the disembarkation point on Bryher.

Straight to the pool behind the hotel in search of a particular bird. The rest of us are either looking in the wrong place or at the wrong bird when someone asks what's that one right under our noses. The lesser yellowlegs we hoped to see of course. An American vagrant foraging in shallow water.

Linnets in light, wavering flight, wrens in bright reddish-brown plumage, rattling and trilling, and the tails of stonechats flickering in time with their rapid warbling song as the wise thrushes perform their rich and fluty songs. These images and sounds around us and the swell of the open Atlantic on one side of this wild little island provide a magnificent setting in which to picnic.

St AGNES

We hulled a while at Hugh Town to see a few of the local sights on St Mary's, before hoisting sail and heading on our way to St Agnes. Shocking magenta, and more like orchids than gladioli, the 'jacks' as they are known throughout the Isles of Scilly, are in the gardens and spilling out into the streets. Echium pininana, or more commonly giant viper's-bugloss, or tower of jewels, are also a ubiquitous plant of the islands. Along the bottom edge of Garrison Hill, up to Star Castle, built in 1593 for the defence of the Isles of Scilly, and into the Wesleyan Chapel which is the Parliament of the Isles of Scilly. Like the sculpted rocks around the perimeter of the island the building is of granite, but cut and worked by man rather than the wind and the sea. And in every crack scurvy-grass is growing in the salt-rich soil. Close to where we embark for our trip to St Agnes is Tregarthen's Hotel, the place where Alfred Lord Tennyson wrote *Enoch Arden* during a visit to the Isles of Scilly.

In the lost land of Lyonesse St Agnes is the most south westerly island of the archipelago known as the Isles of Scilly. Unlike the other islands, which separated from the archipelago around five-thousand years ago, St Agnes has been in splendid isolation in the Atlantic Ocean for closer to ten-thousand years. On one side of the island are her neighbours Gugh and St Mary's. On the other the open Atlantic Ocean.

The sea condition was somewhere between 'smooth with wavelets' and 'slight' when we sailed from St Mary's to St Agnes. 'St Agnes, the oldest and wildest of the islands' was how it was characterised by George Teideman, our guide on the island.

Sea spinach, a blaze of red and yellow bird's foot trefoil, and pink oxalis, surround us as we take the path passing Kallimay Point to the North and around Porth Killier to the Big Pool. On arrival at the Big Pool we find great black-backed and herring gulls bathing, the water jewelling as it rolls off their waterproof plumage. The fixed, repetitive pattern of the preening behaviour, and the shaking of their bodies like wet dogs, appeared to be choreographed, while the softened body contours of the plumage had a tactile feeling transcendent in its beauty. From the somatic to the olfactory and the traces of the seventeenth-century monks of Tavistock, evident in the aroma of the chamomile lawn on the old burial ground. One of the sacred places of the island, peopled in this present moment by a lone bar-tailed godwit among innumerable song thrushes.

The tide is retreating as we look down from the heights of St Agnes to the sandy spit known as a tombolo, the path which will eventually take us over to Gugh. Ragged looking over-sized yellow mesembryanthemum now carpet the way thickly on either side. Their succulent leaves are a cure for warts and they are known locally as hottentot figs. Before crossing over to the smaller island of Gugh we visit the church of St Agnes and learn how it is the setting for some of the greatest maritime disasters in history.

Clean, clear, fresh air is evidenced by the thriving lichen, hairy on the trees; the euonymus japonica shines as we walk, and in amongst all this clarity we find ourselves in a maze made by light house keepers, dating back to the 1700s. As on St Mary's there are more granite stacks on St Agnes, but they are rough-hewn here where the water and wind are not so kind. White and pink campion surround us at the far north-eastern edge of Wingletang Down when we arrive at St Warna's cove. She, the patron saint of shipwrecks, sailed from the south coast of Ireland to the Isles of Scilly in a coracle made of wicker and covered in hides. A natural spring that was Christianised by her presence is known as St Warna's well. Legend has it that pins were thrown into the well and a wish made in order that a ship would be steered away from the treacherous rocks. Or, alternatively, a bent pin was thrown into the water and wishes made for a ship to be guided onto the rocks and wrecked so that the booty could be plundered by the locals.

Olearia hedging or daisy bushes from New Zealand act as a shelter belt along a lane lined with winter heliotrope and pink oxalis. At the bottom of the lane honey spurge and giant periwinkle grow in the gardens of new housing on the island. Trumpet trees, euonymus and red and white valerian mark the end of the lane and the beginning of the grassy plains that lead to the sandbar which is the crossing to the island of Gugh.

GUGH

'Daisies are our silver, buttercups our gold:
This is all the treasure we can have or hold.
Raindrops are our diamonds
And the morning dew;
While for shining sapphires
We've the speedwell blue.'

JAN STRUTHER

The sandbar which provides a crossing point between St Agnes and Gugh at low tide appears Edenic in its tranquillity. The Germander speedwell had spread itself along the edges of the path and across the grassy plains leading down to where the sea had retreated.

Crossing this sandbar aroused an unexpected surge of feeling and took me all the way back to Sunday School.

'And Moses stretched out his hand over the sea; and the Lord
caused the sea to go back by a strong east wind all that night, and
made the sea dry land, and the waters were divided.'

EXODUS 14, 21

There's a spring in my step as I walk the island of Gugh and it isn't just because I'm walking on peat. Bronze age chambered cairns are a seemingly permanent reminder of the temporary. A small copper butterfly basks in the sun on a stone, and tormentil and gorse paint the earth yellow. A waste land of heather roots, a standing stone, the Old Man of Gugh and Obadiah's Barrow. All part of the hypothetical landscape alignments and connections conjured up by the term ley-lines and *The Old Straight Track* of Alfred Watkins.

Meantime time stopped for a time on the blissful Dropnose Porth.

St MARY'S

Early evening on the Garrison. A spotted flycatcher on a rotary dryer. A stunningly creative example of avian ergonomics.

St MARTIN'S

I spent many hours in the field attempting to track down a woodchat shrike. A quiet, gentle amble from the quay on the west side of the island took me from Lower Town to Middle Town, then from Middle Town on to paths through small belts of woodland, the sea now hidden from sight. A copse on one side of a clearing with the gorse bushes stretching across the Plains toward the open sea, seems an ideal place to wait and watch. Having waited and watched I walk on through gorse and scrub and scattered areas of woodland up to the northern-most part of St Martin's. The golden gorse and wild blooming heather give way as I reach the idyllic coast and coves of Pernagle, Plumb Island and Butter Porth. Now, to lie on the sandy beaches by the glistening sea or to persevere with my search for the elusive *Lanius senator*? I opt for lying down with an Auden poem. The first line, 'Look, stranger, on this island now' is achingly apposite. Through Higher Town then over Turfy Hill, back to the coast and down along Wine Cove. Part way along Great Bay the path had been freshly cut through the peat in order to divert it from where some of it had succumbed to the 'pluck and knock of the tide.' The plant life is spectacular between Wine Cove and Great Bay. Here the shocking magenta of the wild gladioli or 'sword lilies' thrive on the sand and gradually create a tunnel, hiding the sea from sight as I walk back once again out onto The Plains to await the arrival of the butcher bird.

> **'Sink into the mire**
> **Embrace the butcher**
> **But change the world.'**

BERTOLT BRECHT

St MARY'S

As I walk through an avenue of lichened trees, wrens burst into song and dunnocks sweetly carol. Male gadwall vermiculations are vivid in the growing light of this last morning on the Isles of Scilly as the flag iris gradually give way to reed beds choked with reeds, and sedge warbler doing more scratching than warbling. This is Lower Moors, part of the nature trail where one week ago I walked my first walk on the Isles of Scilly.

A herring gull's elaborate bathing ritual of head-wetting, wing-shaking and preening, with thirst slaking in between, slows the pace of the day down to what I have grown accustomed to in this lost land of Lyonesse. In the water meadow choked by flag iris a belted Galloway bullock licks the face of a favoured heifer. Wrens' trilling, and the sweet warbling of dunnocks, perfectly in tune with the pace of the island. The dawn chorus of song thrushes rings on in the memory. The Haycocks of Annet, jagged and treacherous. A journey through scrubland and gorse to Porth Hellick Pool. And still I make the road by walking, while great tits practise their infinite variations on themes, though hemlock water dropwort fringes the stream, and the now well-concealed chiffchaffs continue their familiar call, as roots of ivy-clad elm trees trouble the way through Holy Vale.

DAYS OF ABUNDANCE ON THE ISLE OF WIGHT

The inscription on the James Farley Post Office in Manhattan, adapted from an original quotation of Herodotus catches the spirit of determination of Margaret and Lyndon.

'Neither snow nor rain nor heat nor gloom of night stays these couriers from the swift completion of their appointed rounds.'

How quickly we flew to the Isle of Wight from Worcester. Our couriers and carriers, Lyndon the driver and Margaret the navigator. The New Forest, new to me. Lymington to Yarmouth, a journey never undertaken by me before. A stroll along the River Medina was new to me too. And Shanklin Old Village, again new to me; and the Chine and Rylstone Gardens yet to be explored. All of this in one day, is, in retrospect, an indicator of the varied experiences on offer every day of this trip.

Mistle thrushes on berries and buzzards ubiquitous on fence posts as we watch through the sometime drizzle and the sometime veil of rain, but the sun wins through at Wootton Creek where we are detained by a spotted flycatcher. A little later on this day we walk the coastal purlieus of Ryde, where close to fifty ringed plover rest on the beach as around one hundred and fifty sanderling, taking a break from their familiar scurrying over the sand and dodging the waves in search of food, settle in the shadows cast by the resting ringed plover. After such a wonderful surprise, seeing so many ringed plover all at once, together with my favourite wader, the sanderling, everyone is in agreement over a proposed visit to Culver Down. Although the etymology of Culver derives from 'Culfre', the Old English for dove or pigeon, it is at this point that the serious search for the black redstart begins. After a thorough search including strategies such as spreading out and pincer movements, not one redstart is revealed. Raven, but no redstart. And windhover. What an appropriate place for the kestrel to put his name into practice. An uncultivated habitat of dramatic chalk downland and wind in plentiful supply.

The autumn equinox. September 23rd. Newport. The capital of the Isle of Wight. As we pass by the imposing Technical Institute I reflect on how sometimes the majesty of a building has the power to arrest. Onward to Newtown NNR, the chalk downs in the distance. We arrive at Newtown Saltmarsh. Here it's the majesty of the natural world which arrests. Designed by nature, the saltmarsh at Newtown would grace the gardens at Sissinghurst, the delicate web created by the roots of cord grass and glasswort affording a habitat in which both flora and fauna can thrive. Within a relatively small area there's much to admire from the glossy blackberries in the hedgerow to an elegant long-legged greenshank close enough to see his finely patterned plumage as he probes the water-margins for food. Within this marshy enclosure close inspection reveals red samphire, sea aster, sea lavender and sea purslane all at different stages. The Harbour Walk takes us at first through the 'burgages,' numerous plots of land made available to tradesmen and merchants, and past the church at the centre of what was once the most important port on the Isle of Wight. Through the fittingly named Marsh Farm and towards the estuary to arrive at the Mercia Seabroke Hide from where we see an osprey surveying his domain while linnets, swallows and egrets ride the wind. Beyond this point the salt-pan feeder ponds and salt marsh hold turnstone, knot, dunlin, ringed plover and shelduck. From salt marsh to the Coast Guard Meadows for meadow pipits and a flock of Hebridean sheep peaceful among the see-through grass, reddening as autumn advances.

A little later in the day the promised rains arrive and as the Town Hall is closed some of us seek sanctuary in the Church of the Holy Spirit. Just before entering the church I stand intrigued, watching a collared dove, seemingly indifferent to the rain, his head and underparts a pink flush. In the church I find myself intrigued again. This time by a surprisingly small painting of The Infant St John and the Lamb, by Bartolome Esteban Murillo. The craquelure which covers the surface of the painting creates an authenticity and the simplicity of this lively realist portrait lends it great charm. The church itself was light and delicate; a piece of white bone-china edged in blue. The walls were clean and without clutter, the only other artefact on show being an etching of the same image of the child and the lamb. Once more outside I pause again to observe the collared dove. It's difficult to say where his authenticity comes from. Perhaps it's nothing more or less than his simple lived presence.

Shanklin	*up to*	Lake
Lake	*up to*	Sandown
Sandown	*up to*	Brading
Brading	*up to*	Smallbrook
Smallbrook	*up to*	Ryde

A round trip to Portsmouth on a Hovercraft, although there and back again suggested more of a Hobbitcraft. As passengers leave and join at Portsmouth some historic breaking news occurs. So I will always remember where I was when Prime Minister Johnson was judged as having acted illegally over the prorogation of Parliament. This put me in reflective mode, stimulated even further by the name of the hotel encountered when arriving back in Ryde.

Following what was a rainy foray to Portsmouth the two of us reckless enough to battle with the swell returned to the Isle of Wight as the clouds retreated and the warming sun welcomed us to Ryde Esplanade and the prophetically named hotel Arcadia. The beginning of a 'brave new world'? The harmonious wilderness of Greek Mythology, the home of the god, Pan. Well, not a bad model to work towards in my view. And there was something wonderfully Arcadian in the sense of a scene of simple contentment, at the sight of almost one hundred brent geese feeding in the harbour to which Alan directed me, as others went to see whether Sunday's sanderling and ringed plover were still present. The improving light revealed the subtle plumage patterning of these small geese, but the big noise when croaking in chorus eliminated any thoughts of Arcadian peacefulness. Although I missed the kingfisher while enjoying the brent geese, there was some consolation at the sight of two handsome great black-backed gulls, the increasingly common but undeniably beautiful little egrets, and the dipping flight and running, hopping, walking and foraging of the busy rock pipits.

Ryde	*down to*	Smallbrook
Smallbrook	*down to*	Brading
Brading	*down to*	Sandown
Sandown	*down to*	Lake
Lake	*down to*	Shanklin

A fox halts his ascent of a hillock and turns his head as we pass him by in Sandown on our return journey. The promise of red squirrels takes us to Alverstone. An unspoiled wilderness, uncorrupted by civilisation, the wood of oak, hazel, cherry and sweet chestnut has a tranquillity and pastoral simplicity akin to Arcadia. Unfortunately no one had told the red squirrels of this on the day we turned up. For apart from blue tits, great tits, robins and goldfinch, and one spotted flycatcher, this rural idyll appeared somewhat empty.

A visit to Bembridge Harbour gave us a chance to see yet another part of the island where we watched redshank, rock pipit, curlew, black-tailed godwit and oystercatcher. Then further down the coast to Foreland Point where the RNLI lifeboat station, opened in 2010, stood, impressive in its elevation, overlooking the English Channel. The Military Road from Chale toward the unseen Needles, and distant in the mist the white cliffs of Freshwater Bay. A windhover close by, and as we approach Brook Bay a Jersey herd, like Newtown's Hebridean sheep a slightly incongruous but welcoming sight. Passing Freshwater Bay the sea state is moderate, the waves long and breaking with many white caps. And on the land Lyndon alerts us to a guide in the guise of a green woodpecker, escorting us for a short distance before a raven soars into view and we arrive at the Needles car park. Not a pretty sight I hear more than one person say. But then, the beach of Alum Bay with its cliffs and sands of twenty-one differing shades. A natural example of marmotinto, the art of creating pictures using coloured sand. The beach is framed by the chalk stacks known as the Needles, which form the western tip of a band of chalk that crosses the centre of the Isle of Wight, stretching to Culver Cliff in the east, familiar to us because of our search for the black redstart on Culver Down. Beyond the Needles, on the mainland to the west, we look over to Bournemouth and the Isle of Purbeck, the latter a continuation of the chalk ridge running under the sea to Dorset.

It flew across our pathway so quickly it could only be a peregrine, but then it climbed so high, so swiftly, only in retrospect did we have time to speak its name. A peregrine so high it was almost out of sight. Then the wings folded, and down it plummeted into a stoop.

The carline thistles resist the wind. A stonechat shelters in the gorse. From the Needles headland four of us set off for the Tennyson monument, accompanied by another windhover, a true bird of the Isle of Wight. Skylarks rise and undulate alongside linnets, goldfinch and meadow pipits, and a hairy caterpillar, the caterpillar of the oak eggar moth, the first of many, and later the subject of much discussion about Terence Stamp and Samantha Eggar, crawls its way across the island. How strange to look across the Solent over to Hampshire and see Hurst Castle, certainly seen by Tennyson but surely not what he meant by 'The splendour falls on castle walls.' For a moment I'm back at Castell del Rei where the castle which appeared to be growing out of the mountain was much more in tune with a Tennysonian vision. And then the scenery in my mind changes its tune on the appearance of the tanks and stacks of Fawley oil refinery, the largest in the UK, and some say a monument to climate change. Along with other pilgrims we climb closer to the Tennyson monument, many stonechats in, and on, the gorse. One whinchat. Once more the theatre of my imagination is fired up, and as well as the aural proof of Tennyson's onomatopoeic skills echoing from an imagined time, I hear segged brogues striking parquet floor, I hear the cry of the kittiwake, his clarion call, screeching down corridor, ringing through hall. I hear his familiar protestation, 'If I couldn't hear the waves crashing against the shore!' ...... …….. Now, as the waves crash louder than ever before, Basher Grey enters the scene and I'm relishing the richness of some lines from *Morte d'Arthur* in conversation with my three fellow walkers, and it takes no goading for me to recite them:

> 'His own thought drove him, like a goad.
> Dry clashed his harness in the icy caves
> And barren chasms, and all to left and right
> The bare black cliff clanged round him, as he based
> His feet on juts of slippery crag that rang
> Sharp-smitten with the dint of armed heels –
> And on a sudden, lo! the level lake,
> And the long glories of the winter moon.'

Slipping and sliding down the chalky lane where wild clematis, known as old man's beard or traveller's joy, had climbed and entwined itself around any convenient support and the dark flower heads of knapweed and silverweed's silvery leaves lined the verges. Reaching the minibus we watch another kestrel ride a column of air, while under the shade of trees, clumps of hart's tongue fern thrive, their glossy green blades having grown vigorously in the damp atmosphere. A glimpse of the large waves, many white caps and frequent spray of the now crashing sea at Freshwater Bay, then on to Freshwater itself with the surprise of the thatched church of St Agnes. The walk to Yarmouth was along the brackish reaches of the Western Yar estuary. I step onto the footpath into the flightpath of three butterflies, a peacock and two red admiral in quick succession. After a short interval these are followed by a black-tailed godwit, a redshank and a curlew probing the mudflats, mallard and black-headed gulls. Blue and green, a magnificent hawker, the emperor dragonfly holds my attention as it patrols a section of the path then flies up high, losing me in the sky. I come back to earth again when a little egret flies low over the mudflats, where once I imagine a creek used to rise, and now the surrounding grasses and reeds blow rhythmically in the breeze. A solitary swallow flies over and rose hips and the translucent berries of the guelder rose garland the path. In the shelter of the hedgerow four speckled wood flutter in dizzying patterns around one another then settle into stillness as the trilling of a chaffinch warms the air. A small white on an oak leaf, hawthorn vibrant in the hedgerows and the way in which a dead tree lends life to others.

The benefits of travelling in a minibus and with other eyes, is underlined when Lyndon calls out as something crosses the road in front of us. And there on the grass verge he sits before disappearing up a tree. A red squirrel. A few miles to the north west of Shanklin a garlic farm can be found at Mersley. This was a visit which was to have some repercussions, but that's another story. As we depart having made some purchases a kestrel is harried by a carrion crow. No time to hover on the wind for that bird. Through some unfamiliar terrain almost to the north-west corner of the island for another visit to Newtown NNR. As we approach, two Canada geese, wings beating strongly, fly with intent over the Solent. Two kestrels, their 'hurl and gliding' rebuffing the 'big wind' are harried by a crow and a magpie. One retreats, the other retaliates, giving chase to the 'maggie'.

The saltmarsh where we observed so much flora and fauna last Monday is now submerged, Causeway Lake transformed into Swan Lake. A jay on a post marks the way to Walter's Copse and a walk to the East Hide overlooking Clamerkin Lake. From this point, thanks to the eyes of Margaret, Geraldine and Lyndon we see a forty-bird flock of Shelduck as well as female mallard and wigeon in numbers. Common or Arctic tern? A splendid uncertainty here. A diversion to nearby Calbourne to see the thatched cottages of Winkle Street thick with wisteria and a brook replete with water cress. But this fairy tale village also delivers a furry tailed bonus. Where the street comes to an end and the path by the brook narrows, Paul alerts us to a red squirrel which obligingly climbs a tree for all of us to see. This splendid moment was followed by a fine walk from Thorness Bay to Gurnard Bay. Walking our way through smallholdings and arable land toward a coast of mud and sand we see house martins feeding low over a field, swallows all of a rush, starlings perched like musical notes on a pair of staves. Some of us pause by a small pond to look in at the mystery that is fish in their oleaginous kingdom. Carp, and either roach or rudd, we decide after some discussion.

On reaching the beach the first birds to be seen were Mediterranean gulls. Their uniformly pale grey wings and white underparts shone bright and clean in this habitat of mostly muted colours lent by marram grass and teasel, and the mix of mud and sand. A little further along the coast and this proved a beach of great character and variety, another section offering the glorious, but poisonous, yellow-horned poppy. The yellow colour scheme continues with hawkweed and hawkbit scattered amongst the shingle as we walk, watch and listen and a medley of twittering is blown in on the wind followed by a dancing flock of linnets. Two sandwich terns fly along the shoreline before we leave the beach and continue up a lane lined with ragwort, another contributor to the yellow theme. As we approach Cowes some of us leave the minibus to walk a little way along Egypt Esplanade. Six crows, sea-wet backs sleeked and blackened under the sun, scavenge the rock pools at the side of the sea wall. Just off the promenade sandwich terns are feeding and beyond Cowes Harbour the private moorings for the Royal London Yacht Club provide convenient stone pontoons for a group of black-headed gulls and at least one common tern and a Mediterranean gull. A harbour in the proper sense of the word on what is a perfectly calm and beauteous evening. The sea is turquoise, grey, slate blue and sandy with small ripples. The clouds are long and flat, low and fluffy. The air is still and a light heat haze blurs the edge of everything.

The local legend of St Tarquin tells the tale of a dragon that terrorised the village of Brighstone, devouring its children. A once ruthless mercenary knight, St Tarquin, returning from the Crusades atoned for his sins by confronting the dragon. When he pierced the dragon's skin with his lance it shrivelled, turned into wood and laid down roots. Scarred, gnarled and stripped, this lived-in tree an ancient oak with numerous limbs snaking over and around Buddle Brook, re-rooting itself in its reach for life. The Dragon Tree of Brighstone has the ring of a fantasy novel by Alan Garner but is, in fact, one of the trees competing for the title of the Woodland Trust's annual tree of the year competition. On debris of trees through moss and lichen-covered branches behind network of twigs and leaves, a yellow-green rump, lemon-yellow underparts, blue-grey upper parts, a see-saw tail. Perched on a branch, moving through this hidden habitat and spotted by Geraldine. A grey wagtail.

Freshwater Bay revealed two differing sea states when we passed through last Wednesday. But today the breakers are not only white–capping or crashing. Today the ocean swell heaps up the sea so it boils over rocks standing in the way and climbs the cliff face. A slab of grey water, fringes of white in between, and over banks of sand a swelling tide; these are the muted colours and mood of the sea.

Jackdaws ride the wind while we walk the coastal path from Afton Down to Compton Bay. Unlike the jackdaws I'm not in control but picked up and thrown by the wind. And around my feet sea kale and sea cabbage are scattered over the shingle. The delicate little eyebright also thrives in this habitat while bold black berries of wild privet and red berries of cotoneaster surprise. An interlude in Chessell Pottery cafe provides the prelude to rain and a curtain of mist over the sea, but this does not subdue the dazzle of the early evening sun. And the sun wins the first round! But the wind retaliates, whipping from Westside Farm to Walpan and whistling through Whale Chine as even the jackdaws are hurled through the air and we happy few join the meadow pipits, wheatear and windhover, blowing in the wind in an unforgettable climb to St Catherine's Oratory. On the way down a stone carving of Scomber scombrus, the Chale bay mackerel, mysterious harbinger of summer, adds further intrigue to our days of abundance on the Isle of Wight.

A red squirrel, so fast along the ground and up a tree. An evening bonus at Shanklin Chine.

Shanklin to Sandown via Lake. Rain over Sandown Bay. Like us, the swallows gather for departure. One interloper, a sand martin, is spotted by Margaret. A return visit to Culver Down where at last, or at least for some, the talked-up legend becomes reality when Alan spots a black redstart. Three meadow pipits dance in the wind and the rain falls.

The rain has gone and we can see clearly now. Under the sun a kestrel, omnipresent bird of the island, hovers on the edge of the cliff. A walk along the cliff-top road gifts two wall butterflies – or is it the same butterfly twice? In any event an unusual species, confirmed as a certain wall by Richard when he looks at a photograph of its underside. A distant view of a great white egret on Brading Marshes then on to Brading Down where we overlook the semi-circular grass roof of Brading Roman Villa and the River Yar floodplain.

After the natural worlds of Ashey and Arreton Downs we move back in to civilisation with the Hare and Hounds, the Electric Woods and Outdoor Laser Combat pointing the way to the outskirts of Newport, thence to East Cowes with the Italian renaissance palazzo which is Osborne House.

Another osprey, this time one of the Red Funnel's Raptor class ships, returns us to mainland Britain.

PART TWO

ELYSIAN
LOCKDOWN

EARLY DAYS

Late March 2020 and on the spire popularly known as the Glover's Needle a peregrine stands sentinel for the city of Worcester. Since the turn of the year one has been there on most occasions when I have passed by and looked up. Sometimes the bird was braving the rain, and on one occasion a heavy mist shrouded sentinel and city in a damp cloak. As I look up now I reflect on the fact that sentinel is a particularly apposite word given that, as well as meaning to keep watch, it is also, in medicine, an indicator of the presence of disease.

The reference to carpe diem – seize the day – and the gloss put on it by 'everyday there's one less day to seize' in the Isles of Scilly narrative is a manifestation of my love of life and determination to 'drink life to the lees' following a life-threatening illness around ten years ago. Whether a cliché or not, the idea that such an illness may make life feel an even greater gift is, for me, indisputable. Nor was my 'hungry heart' tendency affected too much by the constraints of lockdown.

As one who pays heed to Captain Cuttle's advice, 'When found, make a note of it,' I turn the pages of my diary back to the turn of the year and note that this occasion was also marked for me by the presence of a limping dog fox in our garden at 6.30am on New Year's Day 2020. Was this, I wonder, the presaging of the transformation of our garden into a feeding station for foxes and hedgehogs? Or of some apocalyptic event of even greater moment? Probably neither, but completely unpredictably 2020 seemed to gradually define itself for me as a time to actively experience, and reflect upon, the web of life which embraces the interdependence of humans and the natural world.

When, on March 12th, a group of us left Malvern for a Worcestershire Wildlife Trust trip to Wiltshire, the Cheltenham National Hunt Festival was already into its third day, and Liverpool FC had just hosted a game against Madrid. Although this turned out to be the last such trip for more than a year I can recall only a low level of concern around the coronavirus threat. At that time, apart from a growing awareness evidenced in the emergence of the 'elbow handshake' any threat was, for the most part, treated lightly.

Flint underfoot and lark song overhead as we explore some of the 2,600 acres that is Lower Pertwood Organic Farm, an area which has been farmed for the last 2,500 years. And although it doesn't quite feel like 480 BC it certainly holds something of a time and a landscape now lost. The spirit of it is pre-enclosure, with very few fences and no hedges, just natural shelter belts of trees. This lost-landscape feel is further evidenced by the abundance of birds and mammals as we walk through fields planted with barley, or being fertilised by red cattle. Apart from this, the only signs of Pertwood being a working farm were a couple of tractors ploughing in preparation for planting familiar crops such as barley, or ancient crops like sainfoin, phacelia and fescue. Much of the land was simply left to nature so that an area known as Peewit's Gorse is apparently home to many nesting birds come spring. Stonechats were the only presence around Peewit's Gorse at this time, but we did see other species as we walked the six miles that we eventually covered, at a tempo somewhere between largo and adagio.

Throughout the walk roe deer sat in the sun or ran from hail or rain across the open plains, or down the field edges, sometimes watching us, sometimes showing nothing but a white rump. The overriding impression for me was the sense of limitless, open space. This was enhanced by flocks of fieldfare flying over silently, then a moment in which we strolled down a wide woodland ride, to see two hares watching us from a hillock in the distance. As we approached they sat upright with ears pricked, then took off as we invaded their space. The hoarse croak of ravens above us gifted another moment of being, then, as we walked down a tree-lined lane, towards some old farm buildings, flocks of corn buntings, scribbly jacks and linnets crossed our path from different directions. It made me so dizzy it was like being spun back in time to South Shields and Cleadon Hills when they were the very farm birds that filled my 'young and easy' days. Red to finish. Only one red fox but a fair few red-legged partridge and one magnificent sighting of a red kite as he soared then flew with relaxed wing beats, completely in harmony with the calm of the day.

My personal lockdown began on March 17th as, at first, the garden seemed enough for me. The small tortoiseshell and peacock butterflies, the visiting foxes, late evening and early morning, all 'gave delight and hurt not.' However, on the 23rd I decide to drive the five minutes to Monkwood Nature Reserve for some much needed exercise. On stepping out of the car a brimstone flits over a dried out pool into shafts of sunlight. The primroses look pale in comparison with this fresh lemon-yellow male, the origin of the term butterfly. There are more of them as I take the solitary path along the woodland ride and the primroses are supplanted by wood anemone. Chiffchaffs strike up and are highlighted by a background accompaniment of blue tits' high-pitched trilling and great tits' frantic bicycle-pumping. One, two, three commas, land on the dried mud then move as my shadow falls on them, and I walk until I can get no further without plodging through the clarts. And the buzzards soar as my heart does the same.

Two days later and I am about to walk along the river into the city. On the advice of my older son, Sam, I drive to Grimley gravel pits instead. Like Monkwood, a five minute drive, and probably a safer alternative than a walk into Worcester city. A chiffchaff greets me as I park the car, and as I walk over the still very muddy field towards the two main pools the song of the skylarks, the call of the peewit and the whinnying of the little grebe surround me. I lift the binoculars and a pair of redshank shine under the bluest of skies. A buzzard soars in the big silence while down below the ubiquitous bird is the reed bunting. A perfect view of a green woodpecker reminds me that all of these birds were shining brightly for the coming spring. The plumage of every one of them gleamed. Coots, taking a break from fighting, grazed quietly as a black-headed gull harried a heron, and the air was filled with the calls of chiffchaffs. A peacock butterfly as I walk across the causeway, but only showing the almost black velvet underwings. Off the causeway and over the boggy ground where the willow catkins have fallen and the mare's tails are just coming through. Along a hedgerow and another peacock almost flies into my face then lands on the blackthorn blossom I was admiring. Amongst all of this glory I mustn't forget the waterfowl. They too are clean and polished, gleaming into spring. Shoveler and tufted duck in great numbers, with a few teal and gadwall. But it's the silver-grey back and the ginger-red head of the common pochard which shine on in my memory. 'Common!' Never in the world. Two skylarks, plumage not quite ready for mating, are hunkered down in a field where just beyond them tiny seedless alder cones, left-overs from the autumn, were the only instances of the end amongst these beginnings. Then to lift me once again, the plaintive call of a curlew, flying over as I left.

I wait; I watch this empty space in this 'brave new world,' night's air clean, silent, still; as from nowhere he comes. Watcher's feet planted firmly, mystified still by silence; watched trots silent then still, balancing earth under moon on four black paws, brush fully extended in silence and stillness. Red fox is present. The thrill rivets me in time. And then next night there were two. This smaller intruder, redder and ruder, healthier, cruder, chunkier, hunkier. But is there another? One who walks unknown to stand in the lived moment; or is it a shadow singing, 'or just another song that's in my heart to linger on?' Oh no! A more physically present fox I could not imagine. Not red, more the colour of that coconut coir matting from primary school days in the nineteen-fifties. I can still feel the prickles while learning how to do a forward roll. So yes, the texture too, as I look down on this broad back of bristle and preposterously proud brush.

The end of March approaches and, in what is a glorious spring, I am one of those who is fortunate enough to be able to spend much of my time in the garden. Among my rewards, the gift of a small tortoiseshell, and on the following day a peacock butterfly. Two more days and either a small or large white puts in a welcome appearance. Welcome to me at least, but to many gardeners both of these butterflies are known as 'cabbage whites' because of the efficient job the larva does in decimating cabbages. For me, however, the 'cabbage white' instantly reminds me of my grandfather, who I increasingly begin to think I'm turning into, as I plant dahlias to add more of the past alongside the verbena and dianthus.

> 'Philip', she shouts, but he's lost among his lupins-long
> and preposterous pom-pom dahlias, as flickering fingers
> delve into gloriously trumpeting nasturtiums
> and with well-practised prestidigitation he reveals
> the black and yellow caterpillars lying beneath the leaves.

I hadn't seen him since New Year's Day but, wonderful to relate, early morning of the following day limping his way up the road is the dog fox; limping his way into lockdown and capitalising on quiet, unpeopled streets and roads. And the availability of food. Whether or not he has been supported, in the interim, as a member of a den is not possible to say but certainly there's some evidence of a culture of sharing, emerging between the four foxes.

Over the gardens chiffchaffs call. Amid cowls and caps and spinners, under element digital television aerial, keen grey eyes watch the skies from conning-tower chimney stack. Tail feathers quiver, bills click; jackdaws are in attendance. Sultanas for blackbird and robin every morning as March marches on. In the laurel the blackbird, five greenish-blue eggs, finely spotted with warm brown. Next door neighbours' apple tree for the robin, six white eggs, speckled with light red. Early April, early morning, and a fox is feeding in the garden. An orange tip flashes his forewings then lands on the garlic mustard to reveal his underside and the subtly mottled green of his hindwings.

Two days after the orange tip, another butterfly, the pale blue of the upperside narrowly margined in black. Minute black spots on a silvery pale underside confirm this as a holly blue. And this is not the only one. Over the days that follow it proves to be the first of what becomes something of a localised irruption throughout April. As April progresses the first comma also appears in the garden. And in the early morning two foxes, a young male chasing an older vixen. Playing perhaps? Another first of the year for the garden; a brimstone. The following early morning, two more foxes. One feeds then sits in the middle of the road for a stretch and a scratch. Another sniffs at the food, picks up the container in his teeth, empties it and leaves. A young hedgehog puts in an appearance. Tucks in to what is left and is joined by a fox cub. For one incredible moment young hedgehog and fox cub are feeding together.

Late April. A month has passed since I last stepped out of the car here and there's an orange tip and a large white on the grass verge. On the edge of the pits three oystercatchers as still as the air around them, two redshank feeding fussily and welcoming calls from little grebe, coots and a mute swan, wings creaking as it takes off over the still of the biggest pool at Grimley gravel pits. Along the path lined with calling sedge warblers, one putting in an appearance. A handsome reed bunting sings his part then flies off as a heron watches from the shallows of another pool. Through a gate and into a field over which three larks introduce another element to this splendid symphony. On leaving I note two noiseless great crested grebes focused only on mating, and a pair of mallard who are already taking their chicks for a soothing trip around the smallest of all the pools, in this musical haven where silence and sound coexist.

I saw my first swallows of the year today. The first crossed my field of vision when I was listening intently to a pair of clamorous sedge warblers calling to one another. Then three came into view as I was enjoying the sight of a handsome pochard. One more, over the old barn, as I stalked a pair of green woodpeckers, like the sedge warblers, calling to one another. The flushing of a snipe provided a further highlight; then on leaving, the thrill of hearing the first cuckoo in spring.

Only a day later as April closes and I could not resist a repeat of the five-minute drive, then an hour's walk around the gravel pits. A huge flock of sand martins had me dizzy watching them. At least two house martins in there with them. Walked over to Top Barn Farm where I watched a windhover, then listened to a cuckoo calling. I circled its territory. Got really close, but no cigar. A fledgling thrush making a hell of a din was some consolation. Through a wood of wild garlic where at first, with the noisy scratching and clamouring, I thought there must be sedge or reed warblers present. Then I saw and heard the blackcap, opening his aria with a scratchy recitative. Back to the car via the gravel pits. Happy families. A pair of mallard with twelve chicks. Two coot, and five young, as proud as prelates, sporting red beaks and yellow heads.

Two more days had elapsed and the weather seemed promising so I took me to the pits of gravel. Parked on the road at the beginning of the path down to the Hippo pool and heard the twittering of what looked like house martins. It was raining lightly as I tried to spot the white rumps. The surprise of swifts among the martins distracted me for a while before I could confirm that this was indeed a mix of swifts and house martins. I walked onwards and over the causeway between the two pools as the rain became a little heavier. Over the pool to my right were teeming masses of speeding sand martins, some lined up along the fence wires with a small number of swallows. Looked to my left and the sky was full of swifts and house martins, now much easier to see. All three hirundines, and swifts as well. Arriving at the gate where I had stopped around an hour earlier I stood again and looked back over the pools and the tract of open country across which I had travelled to walk around the cuckoo territory. The sweep of the field under the lark-filled sky had my pulse racing again as I recalled the sight of a lark dropping down just in front of me, then walking to its nest. I was sure I had been watching it carefully but it cleverly eluded me when I focused on what I thought was the lark, and it turned out to be a handsome wheatear. After that I had walked through the wood on the far edge of the cuckoo territory next to Top Barn Farm and watched a mistle thrush rooting around for berries, insects, worms or snails. On the return journey a pleasant warbling tune drew my attention then changed into a rattling, repetitive call. A whitethroat popped up from the depths of a hawthorn then flew into a nearby bush. Definitely a whitethroat. The head seemed more blue than grey. Lesser I think, but I could not be sure. Another case of splendid uncertainty. When I had originally arrived at the gate I was surrounded by a frantically flying group of sand martins and swifts. This second time they had been replaced by a host of house martins flying so close to me I was rooted to the spot.

A cuckoo called, the rain began to fall and the thunder rumbled over the gravel pits where I had earlier stood and watched a reed warbler, its singing ringing over the water. I had planned to finish this outing with a return to the gravel pits, but following all those spring riches I decided it was time to return home. Good thing too, I thought, as I drove back through a hailstorm.

'Pinch, punch, first day of the month.' 'White rabbits' and we're into May. 'Went the day well?' I hear you ask. My reply is that it was one filled with osier, brambles, hawthorn and reeds. The sort of habitat in which I always expect reed and sedge warblers, both of which I can now distinguish by song and by sight.

The whitethroat is another matter, despite how easy the books tell me it is to distinguish between the slightly larger whitethroat and the lesser. I'm working now on listening closely for the skulking lesser.

I didn't recognise them at first as it is not normally until the beginning of July when I see them chasing dragonflies. These two were high up. Amongst the house martins and sand martins. And although they will chase and catch them it wasn't happening on this occasion. Instead they seemed to be more interested in demonstrating their flying prowess to each other. That definitely isn't a kestrel I thought. Or a peregrine. Could it be a merlin? No, far too big. Then I remembered. They are like giant swifts with their long, narrow wings. Hobbies. Also present at Grimley gravel pits are a little ringed plover, a common tern and lots of lovely *vanellus vanellus*, lapwing as they are more commonly known.

A walk over to the cuckoo territory by Top Barn Farm takes me into a different habitat. That beautifully evocative word osier, so often used by the great nature poet, John Clare, might be enough on its own to conjure up the images that remain stubbornly in my thoughts but I believe a mention of oak and ash, keys included, plus a profusion of May blossom will further help to explain what attracted blackcap, whitethroat and orange tips, the male and female of the species, to the corner of a little wood where I could also hear a distant cuckoo calling. On returning to the gravel pits my attention is drawn to two bulky, uniformly grey-brown geese with orange-bills. Frequently regarded rather dismissively as the ancestors of domesticated 'farmyard' geese, the sleek and elegant motion of these two greylag parents, accompanied by their three offspring, is another striking reminder of Browning's astute observation which I applied earlier to the common skua or bonxie.

A little further into May and Grimley was the setting for my first speckled wood on the edge of a small-scale glade, and then for a concert that really pushed the boundaries. The concert was conducted by a heron which took me to a corner of the gravel pits I didn't visit very often. I stood in the presence of the heron who also stood patiently. The coots were squabbling and the reed warblers were singing their cacophonous song. I set up the scope and surveyed the scene. I thought the highlight had come when a reed warbler appeared and climbed up a reed. Great view. Then I thought I could hear what sounded at first like a duck but then spread around the reed bed and increased in volume. That's when I saw the green heads and the inflated vocal sacs and I'm in the purlieus of Ternelles watching some creature with a talent for singing like croaking, laughing birds, attempting to attract females. The only difference was that my beautiful comrades from the North weren't with me, and these marsh frogs were accompanied by reed warblers, coots, and the whinnying calls of the little grebe.

The following day a return to the gravel pits where a little ringed plover stood cheek by jowl with giant geese, greylag and Canada. Crazed coots and beautiful but threateningly noisy lapwings further frustrated his efforts at social distancing. And yet. This was the one that stood out for me. Delicate in every detail; neat collar, sharp black bill, yellow legs and matching eye-ring. A bijou bird who kept his cool. Seductive sirens sing to me. But I refuse to be distracted by the magical sound of those marsh frogs and tie myself to the metaphorical mast of the elusive cuckoo as I sail on through the gravel pits. Once near the wild, garlic-scented wood the cuckoo proves himself to be consistently elusive, so I turn my attention to the aggressive behaviour of a mistle thrush. I listen fascinated to his scolding until I realise that I am the intruder near the nest. Back to the car via the gravel pits where the screeching whistles of the swifts see me off the premises.

HERD INSTINCT

Seven barn swallows. May advances but this is still the biggest group of swallows I have seen this year, appropriately enough hanging around a barn. Through a gate and past five quietly grazing horses. Certainly not thoroughbreds and too timid even to glance at me. I am ringing the changes today. Trying Clifton gravel pits. Through another gate which accesses the path to Croome Park and I'm in a safe haven, surrounded by fields. The main pool is just below an adjacent field. But it's slim pickings. One redshank. And one black-tailed godwit. Quite a few shelduck. But surprisingly, no yellow wagtails, summer visitors usually to be seen snatching at insects stirred up by the hooves of horses and cattle. Then a sound I do not recognize at first; but as it becomes louder, I know. Trot into canter, then gallop; loose limbs' rhythmic spring, and hooves pounding the earth. At first a comforting sound; about ten horses, concerted and controlled in the field adjacent to where I am standing. I look behind and the five I saw as I walked through the first field are no longer grazing timidly but galloping wildly, hooves striking the earth, to join the larger herd. In moments they are one, with one intention and this newly formed herd soon disappears from view. But now there's more, must be another ten. And now they are coming towards me. Even though I know I am perfectly safe with a metal gate either side of me I am frozen to the spot. Then 'heaven blazes in my breast' as they pull up in front of me and one begins to buck and rear excitedly. And now this third group of horses are calming down and, if I didn't think I knew better, I might think they are thinking. A few seconds later one of them turns and trots away from me, finds an open gate and the others follow, trotting then cantering past me and off into the distance. Time to go home, but when I reach the gate to take me back to the car there is a large gathering of horses and a young lad and lass singling some out and putting them in another field. I approach slowly and ask if it's safe to walk through. Yes, is the answer. Turns out that the first ten had broken out of their field and inspired the natural herd instinct in the others. And herd immunity? Questions around whether or not herd immunity can be achieved run through my mind as I journey home. Wherever else the coronavirus is it is certainly in the innermost self.

A short trip from Worcester to Powick then on to the other side of the village of Callow End takes me to some common land which I always think of as the foothills of the Malverns. The closed car park stymies my planned reconnaissance of the Old Hills so I decide to try the Avon Meadows in Pershore. There was instant gratification on my part when I heard the ubiquitous sedge warbler as I approached, then experienced some stunning views of individual birds in the limpid light of the early morning sun. Next was an absolutely beautiful blackcap. It sometimes surprises me, especially when in bright sun as this one was, how the grey seems almost silver and has an amazing sheen. The neat little cap sets it off to perfection. Pure white and plumed, the summer adult little egrets were stunningly present, and as I watched these elegant beings stabbing for prey I recalled that I only ever knew them from the rare birds list in my well-thumbed copy of the 1959 edition of Collins Pocket Guide to British Birds. Throughout my time at the Avon Meadows the cuckoo called. I do believe I shall rise early and spend a bit more time there tomorrow morning.

FEATHERED FRIENDS, FROGS AND FISH

On the afternoon of the same day, with more of a gentle but intense mellowness than a fierce flame, the sun caressed and cajoled. Over recent days the warmth had grown and the green foliage in its varying shades were small stitches of natural needlepoint over a vast canvas.

It was illuminating to have another set of senses with which to survey this canvas. I pointed out birds – little ringed plover, redshank and common sandpiper along the water margins. Lapwings paired up now in wavering flight and calling out their other name. Then, as we listened to and watched those green critters from the planet Marsh, with bulging eyes and inflated vocal sacs pulsing as they sang along with the sedge and reed warblers and the little grebe whinnying away, Sam asked what the bird was at the base of the nearby reeds. A reed warbler! Then another. A mating pair sitting together and seemingly enjoying the entertainment. As well as the reed warbler Sam spotted some fish. Roach and rudd. I knew them by the greenish-olive upper parts blending with the water and the bright red of the fins, but wouldn't have noticed them without him. Then his triumph. A huge carp coasting confidently just under the warm, tranquil surface of the pool as we walked across the causeway on this warm, tranquil day. Apart from a passing osprey nothing much would prey on a fish of such a size. Although, I am reminded of the time I surprised a pair of otters, on the causeway at the other end of the gravel pits, feeding on a fish not too much smaller, which they had hauled out of the water.

The following day I arrived at the Avon Meadows, Pershore, at around 8.30 a.m. This is a wetland that was only established in 2008 and it is in a setting in which the gentle Avon runs along one side and there are a number of footpaths, but you can also walk just about anywhere in the meadows. There is also a boardwalk that winds through the reed beds. I usually walk to the far end of the car park, now closed to cars, and begin with a walk along the Avon, but this time I am drawn into the path on the near side by the welcoming bird song. This was an area of bramble, scrub, osiers and hawthorn, all fairly well advanced for what I assume is still so early in the spring.

So Early in the Spring. Jacqui McShee a capella. The album, Sweet Child. The year 1968. The bell-like clarity of the song resonates still. The purity of her voice, 'I'll sail the seas till the day I die, I'll break through the waves, rolling mountain high', shifts my thoughts to the song-flight that whitethroats often perform, before diving back into the vegetation, or landing in a tree. Three times in a row it occurs as I walk through this haven for common whitethroat, which they appeared to be sharing with some pristine-plumaged goldfinch. A little further along what was now a path leading straight to the reed beds, there were a couple of dead trees, obviously home to woodpeckers, and I could hear but not see a calling bird. A hard repeated 'tack' or 'check' sound but no sweet song was emitting at first from the undergrowth, then from deep in a tree. I waited for some time and it put in a couple of appearances, enough to see that it had beautiful creamy-white underparts and was a neatly uniform brown above. Possibly a garden warbler. Interesting that I have blackcap as silvery-grey and garden warbler as creamy-white, while some bird books go for grey and plain.

I soon reached the reed beds and was walking over the boardwalk when I am suddenly stirred by the desolate call of a curlew flying over. Then, in soothing contrast, I watch a kestrel hovering at the nearby field edge. This seems to be turning into a windhover spring for me. I have now seen so many I forget to mention them. I arrived at a turning where there's a good view into and across the reed beds. It wasn't long before I had seen a sedge warbler. Just before this sighting a cuckoo started up, and continued as I watched and listened to the sweet and sour, harsh and jumbled, medley of the sedge warbler.

Then from nowhere and from silence, the cuckoo. I didn't see him till he started calling again from a tree not too far away. The truly, telling moment of 'being there'.

Territorial Imperative: Avon Meadows, Pershore

Saturday 9th May

05.35. I am completely alone as I drive through a Worcester City which is empty of people. Peregrine stands sentinel on the Glover's Needle. Gulls and pigeons are hunkered down on the roofs of buildings apparently abandoned.

05.55. Avon Meadows, Pershore. My third visit in three days. The gates of heaven open and out of the mist the red-coated fox materialises as a whitethroat's harsh, churring call, and short flourish of song reverberate under a sun redder still than the fox. This small community is extended by a fast flyer, the approaching bird closing its wings at regular intervals and coming down to land in a tree. Its grating chatter continues until the female of the species arrives and they both proclaim loudly that this is mistle thrush territory. Then off they fly together, the silence they leave behind filled at first with a scratchy call, then a sweet, silvery song. The song is echoed by the silver-grey plumage, while the black crown confirms a male blackcap. Onto the boardwalk where it's just about possible to untangle the jumble of contrasting notes, harsh and sweet, which make up the virtuosic song of the sedge warbler, from that of the much simpler and less varied version of the reed warbler. Louder still and louder, the sedge rasping and grating, trilling and whistling, the reed rhythmic and repetitive. Squabbling coots contribute their distinctive 'kowks' and 'kwoots' and moorhens their loud, liquid croaks. Emerging from the cacophony of the reed beds a sound in contrast as delicate as gold leaf; the sound of the

93

ubiquitous reed bunting, their repeated, high, thin song piercing the air. As I begin my circumnavigation of the reed beds another fox appears, a paler doppelgänger of the first, and the habitat opens up to reveal meadows, copses and scrubland now freed from the mist. The fox watches me as I back off and turn my attention to the little egret stabbing into the shallows of a pool. A family of mallard are in the shade, apart from the drake, who is very much in the sun, his sharp white collar separating green-glossed head from chestnut breast. A wheezing note delivered from a tree and followed by a medley of twittering and whistling declares the presence of a greenfinch, while in another tree not too far away, a willow warbler sings his wistful song, somewhat uncharacteristically, from a willow tree. Magpies chatter, cheery chiffchaff call their name monotonously, and the great tit blows up a bicycle tyre.

The tinkling trills of a flock of goldfinch, accompany their bounding, buoyant flight in the happiest of dances, obliterated suddenly by a burst of song and a rapid and vigorous warble with a closing trill, which sails over a sea of buttercups, stretches and spills out of the meadow, and carries the song of the wren all the way to Pershore Abbey. I follow the promise of the song as swallows and house martins gather in their chosen domain. Since the mist lifted, a cuckoo has been calling. Now I think I see him on a distant tree. Yes, I can just see him through the binoculars until a magpie spooks him. Mirabile dictu, he flies toward me, then directly over my head, calling still. His territorial imperative my reflected glory. From Pershore to Worcester the lanes of mayflower are beginning to give way to elderflower and take the eye along the woodland, forming in its sumptuous foliage a naturally sculpted carapace of trees. And whose enclave is this I wonder.

With its characteristic mutability, time feels as if it is alternating between a leisurely, unhurried pace and racing days. Half way through May and I tried the Wyre Forest this morning. Relatively quiet. I was disappointed to see that the wood anemones are virtually finished. A couple of wood warblers were to be heard but not seen. By this time most of them will be brooding. The tree pipits were similarly not to be seen. I could only imagine them launching themselves from treetops then lightly floating down to a chosen perch, but the busy song with its repeated phrases could be clearly heard, especially the characteristic diminuendo of 'seeeee, seeee, see.' The wood ants were everywhere and the pairs of pied flycatchers nesting in the sessile oaks were busily capitalising on this abundance of food. Pearl bordered fritillary were on the wing in some numbers. I saw five, but as it was cold, they were rather restless, and it was difficult to see the underwings. My first grey wagtail of the year, a fine looking male, striking in his mating plumage, was busily foraging along the stony margins of Dowles Brook as I departed.

Driving through the city on my way home I see the peregrine still standing sentinel on Glover's Needle. Back in the garden a common blue butterfly and early next morning a fox feeding. A few days later my morning stroll around the garden brings me to a halt by the swordlike leaves of the yucca. I bend over it with care and wonder what this little yellow clustering is on the edge of a disc-shaped web. As I focus in on the cluster I see that it is beginning to disintegrate as some of its component parts move away from the dense mass of what turn out to be tiny arachnids. These miniature, eight-legged invertebrates are a wonder to me and other family members as well as numerous passers-by. With children and adults alike it is wonderful to see their eyes light up as they connect with the natural world, while still, in nearly every instance, remembering to observe social distancing. Having looked closely under and around the multi-bladed yucca I see that there are actually three of these clusters of cross orb-weaver spiderlings *(Araneus diadematus)*, also known as the diadem spider. As they mature these golden-yellow diadems will develop into striking creatures, their body an orb, surmounted by a cross. The Daily Express saw them in a different light:

'These toe-curling images show HUNDREDS of bright yellow spiders in their clusters – and they are HERE in the UK. Thousands of the almost fluorescent arachnids have been terrifying Brits across the country as they cling to door handles, bins, walls and garden plants. The stomach-churning creatures in question are days-old Garden Spiders, who hatch in their hundreds this time every year.'

Thursday 28th May

It is 04.30. Before I drive through the Wyche Cutting I park and look across to Bredon Hill and the Cotswold Ridge as the sun rises. A few minutes later, having parked in the car park opposite The Kettle Sings I make my way up to Pinnacle and Jubilee Hill. One other walker and a stonechat is the only other life to be seen before I look over to the Herefordshire Beacon to greet the goddess of the dawn at British Camp Iron Age hill fort.

THE BLISS OF SOLITUDE:
THE FOREST OF DEAN

Tuesday 9th June

'For solitude sometimes is best society'.

JOHN MILTON

STRENSHAM SERVICES

Isolated in the car. On a whim I decide to see if I can purchase a portable chair in Strensham Services. I can. And do. On my way back to the car there are very few people to avoid and so I begin to notice the number of rooks, not only in nearby trees, but also perched on buildings and in the car-parking area. Ruling the roost while the jackdaws appear as ladies and gentlemen in waiting. Waiting. All waiting.

RAVEL'S BOLERO

Pianissimo at first, rising and rising in an unbroken crescendo to a climactic fortissimo. Melody, harmony and rhythm all unchanging. In simple terms a long gradual crescendo. Ravel's Bolero had been playing in the car for the last fifteen minutes of the journey from Worcester. Enjoying the minimal change in the music as the world around me changed from now until then, from present into past. A fortified baronial palace on a red sandstone crag commands the passage of the River Wye. Goodrich Castle as it's known. Westbury-on-Severn with its stone-lined waterways known as leats. Terraced cottages lining the river, low lying water meadows and steepling, wooded hillsides. The sad, functionless village pub, a black and white timbered building of the eighteenth century, suspended now in timeless times. Cinderford, once Synderford, an area of iron ore mining and smelting since Norman times, and the impression that the past has on the present is manifest.

CANNOP PONDS

The driver of the Post Office van kept her distance physically but closed the gap of misunderstanding when I asked the way to Connap Pools. So, in a few minutes I was walking from a car park through broad-leaved woodland, chiffchaffs still calling their name, about half a mile to the ponds, where, instead of the imagined mandarin ducks, parents are releasing their children into the freedom of watery delights under the late morning sun.

WOORGREENS NATURE RESERVE

Just a couple of miles away. The canopy appears dense from a distance but as I walk into the forest the sun is filtering through so the light quality is perfect. Not that this perfection makes it easy to see. Seated and patiently waiting on my newly purchased chair I can hear the robins and chiffchaffs, great tits and collared doves, but only the robins come readily into view. What sounds like a boy whistling then takes me to two fledgling nuthatches looking as if they are already in the early stages of mastering the technique, peculiar to the nuthatch, of habitually going head first down trees.

A speckled wood on the forest floor. This delicate species thrives on the combination of shaded woodland and dappled sunlight and a diet of aphid honeydew.

Sessile oaks like masts of a sunken ship in a shallow sea of pteridium. Bracken in tints and shades of green. The large, highly divided leaves lifting upwards and outwards like waves of variable hue, intensity and lightness.

A boar. He's big and bristly and his tusks are protruding from his mouth. I see him after he sees me and he draws attention to himself with a loud huffing sound. He holds his ground and it's then that I notice the area around me. A large part of it is uprooted and the soil is disturbed. A certain sign of the presence of wild boar. It's then that I see two more, but they completely ignore me. Too busy foraging. Foraging for anything they can find. Nuts, berries, carrion, roots, tubers, refuse, insects, small reptiles. Even young deer and lambs.

NAGSHEAD

Two familiar Worcester birders are leaving as I arrive. From at least four metres apart we share thoughts on how relatively quiet everything has been for me in Woorgreens and them in Nagshead.

The silence following the noisy, human rabbiting-on is something splendid as I gather up what I need for a walk around a deserted RSPB nature reserve. The two mile, circular walk through ancient oak woodland originally planted as timber for the Royal Navy's ships also consists of open spaces including heathland, steep inclines and spectacular views.

Wrens are widespread, bursting into song, warbling at full throttle and finishing with their familiar trill. A song thrush who hasn't read his Browning fails to sing twice over. But perhaps it's more to do with being preoccupied by a free-flying fledgling in his care. Immersed in forest sounds and silence, one precious moment offers only the leaf-litter skip-through of a grey squirrel. A solitary roe deer watches me and keeps his distance. One fox similarly has his eyes on me, turning round to look at me with some disdain in case I should stand too close to him.

NEW FANCY

As a famously good place for raptors I did fancy this, but if I am going to manage my return to Woorgreens by eight o'clock I decide I should find somewhere to do battle with my soup. An arboretum just along from Woorgreens serves me well. A very different sort of arboreal world.

THE CYRIL HART ARBORETUM

The first tree under which I stand is a Coast redwood and I'm back in California with my elder son. Across Oakland Bay Bridge and a view of the Golden Gate Bridge. Across the Golden Gate Bridge. Lunch in Sausalito. Lobster and poached egg. Up into Muir Woods. A climb accompanied by 'The Boss' singing *Keep Your Eyes on the Prize*. And the Pacific Ocean comes into view. The one redwood in my presence multiplies. Across the Richmond-San Rafael Bridge. All this in a convertible, Chrysler Sebring, gleaming silver.

Never having been to Chile or Argentina the Chilean Pine or Monkey Puzzle Tree is what it is.

I have dined on food and on birdsong. I have dined on memories, many a marvel, all a mystery. My imagination unlocked.

WOORGREENS ONCE MORE

Having walked from the car park and through the cathedral window – a feature of the sculpture trail – I climb up through Dry Heath Ride towards Crabtree Hill, accompanied by swallows and linnets. It is here that I meet, without standing too close to either of them, the two Worcester birders with whom I spoke at Nagshead. There are now six of them. Altogether there are only nine of us on Crabtree Hill. So spread out that I still feel something of a splendid isolation.

Waiting. All waiting. We wait and we see tree pipits and a kestrel. Some notice a green woodpecker undulating over. Some hear the repeated, 'fine careless' raptures of a solitary song thrush. But on this occasion it is the tree pipit who steals the show. He is an assiduous parent, providing fly after fly and always perching on the same metal-meshed sapling, prey in his bill, before returning to the nest.

The throaty roar of the Norton Dominator or Triumph Bonneville was, for many, a sound of the sixties to which we might aspire. But for those of us who can remember there was also the more avuncular sound of the two-stroke motorbike. And now I hear it once again, so skilfully replicated by the sustained churring of the nightjar. This now the name of what in the nineteen-fifties was also known as a goatsucker, night-hawk or fern-owl, then nesting throughout the British Isles, now confined to a few of the heathland areas remaining in this ravaged, blessed plot.

The interminable churring rising and rising in an unbroken crescendo, all unchanging, is suddenly arrested and in the void of silence and the early gloaming a bird breaks cover then floats, smoothly and silently across the dense heather, dying gorse, and bare, parched ground. Within seconds he's gone to earth but it's possible to be certain it was a male because of the tell-tale sign of the white tips on the long, tapered wings and the outer tail feathers. We wait. In monastic silence we wait.

The churring recurs then stops as abruptly as before. The same bird takes off, now to land in some trees on the edge of the heath. The pattern is repeated and the bird now completes the third side of a triangular pathway, finishing up in a tree directly in front of me. A second bird appears and with swoops and glides intersects the triangle. There appears to be a territorial imperative here as the light fades fast and the two are joined by a third bird traversing the disputed territory and creating a stalemate. All three males still flying with swoops and glides, each attempting to establish territory via flight patterns and sounds, the churring now louder and the sounds given variation by the addition of a soft but insistent hollow, wooden tapping on one note, periodically changing pitch.

And now it's pitch black. Ravel's Bolero and the churring are with me as I return to the car. The mention of Bolero raises an attempt at a joke about ice-skating and a more obscure one about Dudley Moore and Bo Derek.

The long day's journey into night is over. The long day has been a perfect, gradual crescendo.

Tuesday 16th June

Now so familiar, he's become my familiar. Perry Green on Glover's Needle.

Wednesday 17th June

I took up my favourite position for watching the hunting hobbies, next to the field gate opposite Tinkers' Coppice. In the absence of hobbies it was one of the two remaining young redshanks that drew my attention to an alternative spectacle, last seen on Bardsey Island. A sudden noisy flight from the crowded water's edge took him to a fence post on the causeway by the Hippo Pool. The parent birds followed. But still the gathering of black-headed gulls, and the cormorants hanging out their wings to dry in the sun, appeared fixated by something. And this something turned out to be the gathering of increasingly excited and noisily piping oystercatchers, who were the cynosure of all eyes, including those of the lapwings, circling and swooping in noisy excitement over the growing group of birds, piping louder than ever now. The lapwings called repeatedly, the redshank family flew back and forth, and the black-headed gulls appeared stunned into silence while the cormorants watched indifferently as the oystercatchers performed their mysterious ritual, many paired up and running backwards

100

and forwards, bills pointed toward the ground, their calls carrying over the purlieus of Grimley gravel pits as this ceremony, probably of courtship or territorial encounter, unfolded in its mystery.

'A growing passion,' is the slogan, punning on the attraction of the place and, the essence of any nursery, nurturing growth and development. I have been here once before and this return half way through June feeds my growing passion for gardening and allows me to try again with some wild flowers. The resounding success of my first attempt was black knapweed, which I am now having to keep under control. This presents no difficulty and reaps the reward of common blue, meadow brown and small and large white butterflies. Beyond that there is still the promise of late summer providing some extra feed for the goldfinch to supplement the sunflower hearts to which they are accustomed. Despite the 'hard-headed' success of the black knapweed and the apparent failure of the bird's-foot trefoil, devil's-bit scabious and ragged robin, I decide to say to the devil with the scabious, but to try again with the bird's-foot trefoil and the ragged robin, together with some new additions.

As August moves into September the wilding is properly out of my control. The original bird's-foot trefoil and devil's-bit scabious have successfully established themselves and only the ragged robin has not returned. Of the new batch the field scabious is now sharing space with the ox-eye daisies which have flowered throughout the summer to take pride of place among the wild ones. The purple betony, and, remarkably for a plant expected to last only until midsummer, the new candy floss pink, ragged robin, put on a fine show until the end of summer. The new bird's-foot trefoil has now extended the 'eggs and bacon' attempted takeover, while the selfheal, which the bees and butterflies are still visiting, has covered and kept its ground. The only threat, which the bird's foot trefoil seems to be resisting, is the mysterious appearance of the rampaging wood avens, possibly attributable to the uninvited presence of the devil's-bit scabious. Also known as herb bennet, the wood aven's mission, derived from the flowers' association with St Benedict in the fifteenth century, is to ward off evil spirits. Meanwhile the marjoram and lady's bedstraw have happily shared a private little plot with a mature magnolia. Only the tansy, placed strategically next to the new lockdown composter as a threat to the bluebottles, failed altogether, though the fault was all mine after I attacked the greenfly with too much Fairy Liquid and deprived myself of the pleasure of seeing the golden button-like flowers in late summer.

Saturday 20th June

On my first visit to Hartlebury Common the whitethroats were popping up from the brambles and briars but were subdued by the early evening rain. Not so the dog-walkers. And so the summer solstice proved something of a washout. There were, however, on returning home, some consolatory avian references in Shakespeare's King Edward III.

The 'golden wings of fame' (1.47) whisk me back to my flight of fancy with Basher Grey.

Then a metaphor from Aesop's fable of the jackdaw borrowing the peacock's feathers:

> 'I'll take away those borrowed plumes of his
> And send him naked to the wilderness' (1. 85-86).

Shakespeare's capacity to notice human parallels in the natural world is employed in a typically vivid and imaginative image. The lowest in the social order of the beehive, which contributes nothing and steals the honey produced by other bees, is contrasted with the king of birds. The speaker is King Edward III, the drone is King John of France.

> 'like the lazy drone
> Crept up by stealth unto the eagle's nest' (1. 94-95).

And finally I'm immersed in references to a bird well-known for its prowess in singing, but in classical literature much more:

> 'That with the nightingale I shall be scarred' (1. 111)

Proverbially, the nightingale kept itself awake and singing all night by leaning its breast on a thorn. There's an astute understanding of the natural world in Shakespeare's chosen imagery and diction which is both charged with dramatic force and apposite to the human condition. In the case of the nightingale this is further developed in Scene 2. 272-6

> 'Her voice to music, or the nightingale –
> To music every summer-leaping swain
> Compares his sunburnt lover when she speaks.
>
> And why should I speak of the nightingale?
> The nightingale sings of adulterate wrong …..'

The nightingale is a bird renowned for its vocal bravura, its warbling, trilling, bubbling, whistling, gurgling cadenza is rich in melody and awesome in its volume. Edward is reminded, however, of its association with Philomela, who is raped by her sister's husband and eventually turned into a nightingale. The most comprehensive version of the myth of Philomela, Tereus and Procne is in Ovid's Metamorphoses, Book VI.

Throughout the last two weeks of June the swifts have established themselves, screaming over the rooftops and scything the sky every evening. This evening of the summer solstice is no exception, and as I depart the world of literature and re-enter the real world of my garden, there they are.

Urban Devils

> Nearer they draw,
> swift, ephemeral, dark;
> some now screaming over the roof tops
> targeting me with teasing pincer movement,
> others envelop then abandon their quarry,
> flashes of inspiration flickering electric
> along the edges of this fool's field of vision;
> dark, swift, ephemeral,
> shaping their own meaning,
> so many and so mysteriously,
> filling my head and stilling my heart
> to look up and see
> those with the hubris of Icarus,
> crowd the sky and fly for the sun,
> ephemeral, dark, swift.

Tuesday 23rd June

Observing the conventions of social distancing a morning walk with Dave was at first among oaks and the few elms which remain in the rolling foothills of the Malverns, commonly called the Old Hills. This is the time of year for purple hairstreak and white-letter hairstreak so I Keep my eye on the canopy as we walk. Fortune does not smile on this approach, but in combination with listening the rewards proliferate. At first a few swallows, then the cheerful, rattling song of the chaffinch, blending with the vibrato of skylarks and chiffchaffs serenading with echoing repetition. All flourishing in entente cordiale. A red admiral, my first of the year, in the partial shade of a glade, which takes us into the meadows adjacent to the Old Hills; marbled white and ringlets a divine disclosure along with the multitudinous meadow brown.

On the evening of the same day a visit to Penny Hill Bank, like the Old Hills a twelve minute drive. This one into silence. Cotton grass and a hawk hanging still. Bird's foot trefoil. Wild strawberry. And the little faces in the yellow-wort to mystify me. Like Vosper's Salem or Anthony's clouds an example, perhaps, of pareidolia.

Through a meadow full of bird's foot trefoil and a few more yellow-worts, to see a dizzying profusion of meadow browns and marbled whites. Negotiating my way in the humid heat, across the sloping contours of this field teeming with life, I am dizzied further in my struggle to get a closer look at a restless small skipper. And it's then I come a cropper. As chance would have it I part company with my wrist watch but fall safely. Within seconds a ringlet lands on my watch and we while away the time together. From a supine position I can relax and appreciate what seems like a little piece of velvet in contrast with the cold steel of the ringlet's landing pad. The dark chocolate brown wings trimmed with white become the cynosure of my eyes until my ears guide me to the sound breaking the unique silence of this evening atmosphere; the sound of a song thrush at full throttle.

Returning home my wife Jacky tells me that she saw an 'orange butterfly' over our garden just after I left for my Penny Hill Bank excursion. For a while I couldn't think what it could be. The following day provided an ocular reminder. Out of the blue, a silver-washed fritillary.

Thursday 25th June

The Malvern Hills. At a distance with Derek, a welcome breeze eases an anti-clockwise circumnavigation of North Hill, via Lady Howard de Walden Drive. As ever the talk is of music. Although we have already shared views on Dylan's *Murder Most Foul* and *I Contain Multitudes* via e-mail, some time is given over to the subject matter of the former, the Kennedy assassination, and to the multifarious cultural references in each. Discussion around Dylan's allusions to specific films and songs leads to Derek's mentioning an album by Midlake, *The Courage of Others*.

I have never heard of Midlake but when Derek mentions one song

'Core of Nature' which takes its theme and title from a poem by Goethe, I know exactly where I am. And I mean exactly where I am in the physical geographical sense, but also, when I reflect on this later, on where I am in relation to the concept.

Back in the natural world but still not far from music as a handsome singing stonechat, buzzards mewing in the blue, and then a minute rose-pink petalled flower all catch my attention. There is something splendid about this tiny plant although I am uncertain as to its identity. Which denizen would choose such a bare and gravelly place? Sand spurrey suggests my copy of *The Wild Flowers of the Malvern Hills*. I send a photograph to Margaret and she confirms it.

Friday 26th June

I didn't intend to do any walking today. But the sun was shining, the sky was clear, and the swifts were screaming.

Ninety minutes I spent in the sunlit glades and walking along the open rides between the trees, including oak, beech, ash and alder, plus small-leaved limes and wild service trees. The riches of the Elysian Fields here in Monkwood. A large colony of white admirals have now taken over from the wood whites and seem to be everywhere. As numerous as the restless meadow browns. Comma and peacock appear together to bask in the sun. They both look so fresh they must have just arrived in this, for them, genuinely 'brave new world'. The small and large skipper look positively drab next to these new-born beauties. One ringlet and one holly blue on the woodland edge, then a speckled wood making its way into the wood. On the path a dark beauty. Not another peacock showing his dark brown/black underside. No, this one's wings are open and he is showing his upperside. Black with iridescent purple. My first ever purple hairstreak. I turn to leave. A muntjac pauses. I pause. In a moment of being we see one another.

Sunday 28th June

Excerpts from an e-mail exchange with cousin Pam.

CP

Surely it'll be safe to be out and about by then. Besides, I can't see folk accepting a return to lockdown.

ME

Now you've gone and done it again. This statement, together with other stuff on my mind has really set me thinking. Just been reading the Introduction to Edward III with Richard Proudfoot and Nicola Bennett doing an excellent job of closely analysing the dramatic efficacy of Edward's passion for the wife of his friend and supporter, the Earl of Salisbury. 'Spurred by his desire for the Countess of Salisbury his will becomes his imperative' (p.24). Interesting to consider the monarch's wilful imperative in comparison with the intuitive territorial imperative of the natural world. Earlier than that, on p.16, there was one sentence that had a particularly resonant currency. In writing about the historical context of the play the editors refer to the 'unmitigated disaster' of the English expedition to France, during The Hundred Years War, pointing out that:

'The few English survivors who straggled back brought a fresh infection of the plague to England.'

This had me reflecting on how the Black Death and The Great Plague was not a myth, and not an epidemic, but a pandemic. We have experienced, or I should say are still experiencing, a pandemic. When I consider what is happening in Brazil, in Germany, in the US and of course here, there seems to be an uncertainty looming and I'm not confident that this uncertainty is likely to be splendid. However, it's still 'nil desperandum young Chambers.' My life goes on positively. And tomorrow I am meeting Margaret at a distance again as she has requested that I show her where the sand spurrey grows.

Monday 29th June

00.45 Juvenile red fox, pale and slight of brush, crosses the road cautiously and disappears into the garden of one of the houses opposite. Thirty minutes later he stands on the threshold of the same garden before re-crossing the road and entering our garden. I think he's come to eat. But he has other ideas. At first he sits, then he sprays a nearby shrub before a cursory sniff of the food provided. That done, he departs. At 02.30 I look out of the window again just in time to see him finish the food then sit down to relax before going back over the road for the next course.
Later that morning I park the car in a lay-by at West Malvern where the conventions of distance-keeping are observed when Margaret arrives in

her car. The two of us make the ascent to the network of paths between Sugarloaf Hill, Table Hill, North Hill and Worcestershire Beacon. Now, which one was it for the sand spurrey? Almost two hours later no result. However, the meadow pipits, stonechats and whitethroats were all showing well. And all with juveniles in tow. Around these birds low-standing bilberries provided a feast for the wood pigeons, as well as taking me back to one particular Sunday afternoon when the family circle assembled at my Nana's. As ever she prepared the table in the presence of the family and our cups overflowed. But on this occasion as well as *divine* snow cake, cheese straws and coconut haystacks, there was also bilberry pie, and, to the delight of the younger family members, concomitant blue fingers, blue lips, blue teeth and blue tongue.

July begins and at Grimley gravel pits the little ringed plover is feeding along the water's edge. Strange how it is often the smallest of birds which one notices. But then something of a group identity grabs my attention. Two young redshank, a lone oystercatcher, an undeniably handsome common tern, and a black-headed gull constitute a company of Red Legs. Just for a moment I am transported to sometime in 1862 when a group of border scouts was formed during the American Civil War to aid the Union cause. The men composing the company became known as Red Legs because they wore leggings of red or tan-coloured leather.

Reed bunting, reed warbler, skylark and sedge warbler all appear to be raising second broods. Disappointingly only a few swallows are in evidence. However, it is wonderful to see so many swifts. Meanwhile the broad-bodied chasers are becoming more numerous every day. A hobby presence feels imminent.

The second day of July. Still supporting, protecting and guiding, Perry Green is on Glover's Needle.

VIRGINIA

An e-mail to cousin Pam.

Life is still good. A beautifully tranquil walk with Dave along the Avon this morning. Started in Tewkesbury and in a couple of minutes it was like being in the opening shot of *Mr Turner*, but with two old males keeping their distance rather than two young milkmaids in a huddling stroll. A lone oystercatcher flew over our heads and piped us in as the banks of cloud piled high all around us, echoing the varying shapes of the crowns of the tree canopy. In spite of the cloud, the intense light combined with the interplay and juxtaposition of the concave and convex surfaces, giving a particularly strong sense of three-dimensionality to the picture. A picture which included a solitary swallow in the near distance, skimming low across the riverside meadow, sweeping it systematically for low-flying insects. Further away, in a field in front of a house strategically positioned on a hill, a clamouring parliament of rooks went about their rookish business. Rookish business which takes me to Virginia. You mentioned that something's been keeping me quiet. I think it was some<u>body</u>. And I mean Virginia. Loving Orlando this second time around. Described by Jorge Luis Borges as Woolf's 'most intense novel, and one of the most singular of our era.'

'Sunk for a long time in profound thoughts as to the value of obscurity, and the delight of having no name, but being like a wave which returns to the deep body of the sea; thinking how obscurity rids the mind of the irk of envy and spite; how it sets running in the veins the free waters of generosity and magnanimity; and allows giving and taking without thanks offered or praise given; which must have been the way of all great poets, for, he thought, Shakespeare must have written like that, and the church builders built like that.'

Friday 3rd July
01.00 Under waxing moon a well-fed fox, black ears and black tail, licks the platter clean. Every corner of his familiar feeding receptacle is scoured with an appreciative tongue. If he could talk what would he say? He doesn't need to. He says it all anyway.

Saturday 4th July

An e-mail to cousin Pam.

'We must shape our words till they are the thinnest integument for our thoughts.' (p.166). I read this last night and was reflecting on Virginia's profound understanding of the power of poetry. Then this morning I read from p.165, 'It was a little book bound in velvet ....' I'm re-tracing my steps now as by the time I turned over the page and read the four words 'faith of her own' I realised this was some sort of epiphany for me. About poetry but also about lived experience. It was Virginia's 'the eye of faith' in combination with her reference to 'of all communions this with the deity is most inscrutable' which made me realise how brilliantly she used reflection to interrogate the sense of the changing self. It was then that I realised I was using this as a springboard for my own reflections. Next came the epiphanic moment when I read the amazing consideration of the minutiae of 'the blood-stain, the lock of hair and a crumb of pastry' to which Orlando added, 'a flake of tobacco, and so, reading and smoking, was moved by the humane jumble of them all – the hair, the pastry, the blood-stain, the tobacco – to such a mood of contemplation as gave her a reverent air.' There is something truly remarkable how these seemingly trivial objects can shift the emphasis into reflections on things spiritual. A uniquely Virginian leap of faith. Then that's where the page turns and Virginia reveals that, 'Orlando, it seemed, had a faith of her own.'

Cousin Pam's response was to send this Kathleen Raine poem:

> 'My day's plan to write
> From gospel text on heaven,
> But saw a wren flit
> And then another, among jasmin
> By the window, and forgot
> Holy pages while in leaves unwritten
> Messengers from the Kingdom.'

I reply with Dylan Thomas' *Fern Hill* and these words:

Interesting how Kathleen Raine's poem and Fern Hill both look at the natural world with 'the eye of faith.' I remember in my first year as a student at Worcester Teacher Training College writing an essay on the History of Education. I wrote it from a highly personalized point of view and the criticism levelled at me was, 'But that is just your perception, how you see the world.' I was aware then, thanks to Basher Grey, that some of those who taught the Arts were, to use Virginia's glorious diction, driven by the 'humane jumble' of a subjectively lived life into a mood of contemplation where 'a faith of one's own' was, without necessarily tracking with the usual God, 'a useful support mechanism.' Well, I say 'I was aware then' but that may be more of a retrospective awareness. It's as if I was only partly conscious then, while now Virginia's words make me tingle with the thrill of existence, the thrill of how I inhabit the world. Not unlike Orlando, through the eye of a faith of my own. And yet, whatever that faith is, probably what mostly ensures fulfilment of my needs is the knowledge that I can always go to my bookshelves, for 'another sip of the divine specific.' Or, of course, out into the natural world. That evening, under the full moon, a new fox on the block. It's only 10.45 and this is a very young-looking fox, hanging around our garden. Nervy. No food out as yet so he trots, stops and looks, then trots, stops, looks and leaves. The following day is a Sunday and I am standing in the graveyard of the church of St Mary, Kempsey watching two swallows skimming over the grass, growing on earth that had not yet been occupied. From the graveyard to Kempsey Common and it's surprising to me how empty such a vast expanse of space can be. Not many years ago I have seen barn owls, short-eared owls and tawny owls here. At present the green veined white butterflies are omnipresent. The small tortoiseshells too are out in numbers. Otherwise it's as ominously quiet as the graveyard.
Just down the road from Kempsey the ladies bedstraw is flourishing at Croome Park. And at this time of year this is a place where butterflies outnumber birds. Marbled white all over the black knapweed, meadow brown all over, and a few velvety ringlets. And gatekeepers too. Happy to flaunt their orange upperside and double pupilled eyespot. Even more small tortoiseshell here. But where are the

painted ladies? I line the camera up with a six-spot burnet moth, a small skipper and a marbled white sharing the common ragwort. I breast a hill and there's the biggest butterfly ever. No, that's a falcon. Scimitar wings. Like a big swift. A hobby? Possibly, but a peregrine would explain why there are so few birds around. A kestrel? So pale. So ephemeral a moment.

I'm back at Grimley gravel pits where I am reminded how amazing it is that such a relatively small space can hold such a variety of birdlife. Reed buntings, reed warblers, sedge warblers, pied wagtails, skylarks and starlings. Then the Red Legs from *The Outlaw Josey Wales* – common tern, redshank, oystercatcher and black-headed gull. A lone dunlin. Another film – *The Usual Suspects* – comes to mind as I notice mallard, coot, tufted duck, Canada geese, graylag geese and mute swans. Plus grey heron, little egret, cormorant, buzzard and kestrel. And of course our special guests – swifts, swallows and house martins. Then suddenly, just before I leave forty plus lapwings turn up. Now where did they come from?

Monday 6th July

Monday 6th July

Monday 6th July

Speckled wood and marbled white in our garden.

An e-mail to cousin Pam.

Following the Archduke/Archduchess episode I thought Virginia was on top form in her passion for Vita. There was something sumptuous in the warm love of 'a morning gown of sprigged cotton,' 'dove grey taffeta,' 'peach bloom' and 'wine-coloured brocade.' Then the looking-glass ritual – 'she was like a fire, a burning bush, and the candle flames about her head were silver leaves; or again, the glass was green water, and she a mermaid, slung with pearls, a siren in a cave singing so that oarsmen leant from their boats and fell down, down to embrace her; so dark, so bright, so hard, so soft was she.'

Virginia's writing on 'Orlando the man and Orlando the woman' reveals a 'modern' and knowing sensibility in this area, which in Virginia's hands becomes both witty observation and a genuinely philosophical and psychological exploration into what she refers to as a profound difference between the sexes. 'Clothes are but a symbol of something hid deep beneath' (p.180) and 'Different though the sexes are, they intermix. In every human being a vacillation from one sex to the other takes place, and often it is only the clothes that keep the male or female likeness, while underneath the sex is the very opposite of what it is above.' (p. 181). This is pretty daring stuff from a young woman. The seriousness of such challenging subject matter is all the more impressively innovative because it is also playful and life-enhancing – how outrageous but prescient is Virginia's creation of Orlando as someone who has the experiences of not being male or female, but being both! A remarkable achievement and that's with only a fleeting mention of the superlative poetry.

Tuesday 7ᵗʰ July

Perry Green on Glover's Needle.

Wednesday 8th July

An e-mail to cousin Pam.

> Just thought I would mention that I am still enjoying a very slow immersion in this journey with Virginia. Some of yesterday's words:
>
> > 'Thus the British Empire came into existence; and thus – for there is no stopping damp; it gets into the inkpot as it gets into the woodwork – sentences swelled, adjectives multiplied, lyrics became epics, and little trifles that had been essays a column long were now encyclopaedias in ten or twenty columns.' (p.219).

Then some of last night's words having listened to another master of diction and imagery. 'A man of contradictions', from *I Contain Multitudes*. 'An enemy of the unlived, meaningless life', from *False Prophet*. 'Let all of your earthly thoughts be a prayer', from *Black Rider*. 'I can't sing a song that I don't understand', from *Goodbye Jimmy Reid*. 'See the light that freedom gives', from *I Crossed the Rubicon*. 'Falling in love with Calliope' from *Mother of Muses*. 'I got up early so I could greet the goddess of the dawn', from *I Crossed the Rubicon*. 'Beyond the sea, beyond the shifting sand', from Key West. All lyrics from *Rough and Rowdy Ways*.

I stepped out of the shower this morning enriched and inebriated on words. The eloquence, the mystery, the music. Then the ecstasy of a gift at Grimley gravel pits.

Looking up, I stand outside myself and notice. A hobby. Lived life in a dead tree, dining on a dragonfly. Appetite sated, off he goes on a wing and a prayer.

'Isn't that a kind of prayer? The care and maintenance of the web of our noticing, the paying heed?'

KATHLEEN JAMIE

Looking down, I stand outside myself and notice. Waders in the water. Dunlin and common sandpiper have now joined the redshank. All waders in the water. One of Jacky's favourite gospel songs comes in on the ocean swell of association.

> 'Wade in the water, wade in the water children,
> Wade in the water,
> God's gonna trouble the water.
> You don't believe I've been redeemed,
> Wade in the water,
> Just see the Holy Ghost looking for me,
> God's gonna trouble the water.
>
> Wade in the water, wade in the water children,
> Wade in the water,
> God's gonna trouble the water.'

Thursday 9th July

I agree on Virginia & Vita's dislike of the Victorian era. This section read not only as a time of social change but also as a time of climate change. From the all-pervasive dampness to 'dolphins dying in Ionian seas' (p.221) it's as parlous and uncertain for sensitive souls as the times in which we find ourselves. But with Virginia empathy abounds.

Fantastic understanding of those times and edifices, both concrete buildings and abstract values. 'It looked as if it were determined to endure forever ..... so prosaic, so matter-of-fact, so impervious to any hint of dawn or sunset, seemingly calculated to last forever.' (p. 223). Echoes of the British Empire, of the Ruling Class, of Paternalism, and of 'the Victorian insistence on motherhood as the only function of femininity' (note on p.224).

There was a culminative moment for me when I felt the unfettered joy and celebration of living in the natural world with which Chapter VI seems to tremble and explode in ecstasy. I knew there was something special happening as Orlando's looking out of the window (p.278) shifted to the 'frail, reedy, fruity, jerky' old barrel organ sound. Then 'the music of the spheres' and the 'gasps and groans' presaged something special. My first thought was that this needed to be read out loud.

Then it all made sense. Orgasm and birth simultaneously evoked by Virginia's words. At first the fecundity of Kew Gardens (p. 279) – '... ..under the plum tree, a grape hyacinth, and a crocus, and a bud, too, on the almond tree; so that to walk there is to be thinking of bulbs, hairy and red, thrust into the earth.....' Then all of the wondrous, recurrent imagery of mystery in the everyday world, of 'divine happiness and pleasure of all sorts' (p.280) peppered with images of the promise of the kingfisher, and culminating in its coming:

> 'Blue, like a match struck right in the ball of the innermost eye, he flys, burns, bursts the seal of sleep; the kingfisher; so that now floods back refluent like a tide, the red, thick stream of life again; bubbling, dripping; and we rise, and our eyes (for how handy a rhyme is to pass us safe over the awkward transition from death to life*) fall on – (here the barrel-organ stops playing abruptly).'

> 'It's a very fine boy, M'Lady,' said Mrs Banting, the midwife, putting her first-born child into Orlando's arms.** (pp. 281-2)

---

* This may suggest 'la petite mort' – the sensation of post orgasm as likened to death. It can refer to the spiritual release that comes with orgasm or to a short period of melancholy or transcendence as a result of the expenditure of the 'life-force'. Roland Barthes spoke of la petite mort as the chief objective of reading literature, the feeling one should get when experiencing any great literature.

** The rhythms of the writing create a vivid sense of the phenomenon of orgasm as well as a vivid sense of life beginning.

Met Charles and Caroline (aka Chas and Caz) at Grimley gravel pits. Probably too much hope invested in the reappearance of the hobby. Despite that omission it is always a joy to be with two people who have such a deep affiliation to the natural world. Caz spotted a kite as soon as we started the stroll down Tinker's Coppice towards the Hippo Pool. That particular habitat clearly delighted Chas, who took the profoundest pleasure in the pruinous blue abdomen of the broad bodied chaser.

ODE TO JOY: HARTLEBURY COMMON

'Joy, bright spark of divinity,
Daughter of Elysium,
Drunk with fire we tread
Within thy sanctuary.
Thy magic power re-unites
All that custom has divided,
All men become brothers,
Under the sway of thy gentle wings.'

Arriving in the car park at Wilden Top I step out of the car to find a bijou blue jewel of a flower. This is the germander speedwell – the 'shining sapphire' of Jan Struther's 'speedwell blue' in the children's hymn, 'Daisies Are Our Silver.' A few hours later, when I am just about to leave, it is the ragged but handsome daisy-like flowers of the common ragwort which engage my attention. Its large, dense, flat-topped clusters of yellow flowers are striking, but it is something about the leaves that I notice; writhing on these leaves, in their black and yellow hooped jerseys, the caterpillars of the cinnabar moth.

From Wilden Top car park an undulating path through gorse and scrub, with the occasional mountain ash, takes me along the first part of a butterfly walk to a sturdy five-bar gate. Away from the road, behind this gate and below an embankment along the edge of a wood, lies the largest area of heathland in Worcestershire. This is a habitat of scattered woodland, holloways, quarries, swathes of dry, sandy areas and pools; all of which owe their existence to man. This wild and ancient landscape has a mystique memorialised by Shakespeare with *King Lear's* 'blasted heath,' and by Thomas Hardy in *The Return of the Native*, where Egdon Heath is a symbol for the cosmic world of mankind. Heathland, a product of the clearing of forests on acid, sandy soils, is a habitat the character of which is determined by grazing, cutting and burning. Heathland, something stripped back to its essence; something pagan; and with an atmosphere permeated by custom and superstition.

It seemed that out of lockdown I escaped down some profound, bright tunnel in green shade of bracken and grey of dying gorse, lit by the berries of 'the bead-bonny ash.' Cooped up in this scooped out holloway my senses settle and I notice two sources of sound. One is the fledgling robins chorusing with the family of blue tits, searching for food in the elevated oaks as chiffchaffs tirelessly reprise their eponymous name. The other sound source is, at first, something of a mystery, the occasional sharp crack making me turn my head in surprise. Then I see what I hear. The seed pods of the broom are bursting under the sun, shedding seeds on what, judging by the walls of broom, is certainly not all stony ground. Before leaving this little haven I stand in the lived moment a little longer. It is then that I realise that I have given no more than a curt glance and logged as black what is a perfect purplish sheen. These iridescent carapaces also make music, rattling as the wind picks up.

I walk a little further, the heath opens out and overhead power lines loom above the sandy path. It is in this none too salubrious setting that I park my portable chair to eat by scrub and shrub. A peacock butterfly perches on the path, wings closed to reveal its almost black undersides. As the sun comes out from behind a cloud the wings flick open to reveal a brightly coloured eyespot on each of its four wings, while two whirling dervishes of the air pause for a moment to reveal the coppery metallic sheen of their black spotted orange forewings. Small copper butterflies. In this man-made mystery the miniscule sand spurrey is easily missed. The five rose-pink petals of this star-shaped flower are slightly shorter than the five green sepals that separate them. As I lift my eyes from looking down at this tiny gem, small white and large white butterflies come into view and a holly blue closes its wings on landing, to reveal its silvery pale blue underside with tiny black squiggles. Gatekeeper, velvety and vivid orange, meadow brown and ringlet, make up a trio of height-of-summer butterflies as I leave the humming powerlines and take the sandy path which widens and deepens as I climb up the escarpment to experience yet another perspective on this heath. This is a perspective that fires up my imagination and helps to explain the compelling mystery of such a place. The oak I see up here on the edge of the escarpment has grown as if to accommodate itself into the frame of my camera. It fills the frame with stunning precision. The branches are all about the same length, the crown goes down to the sandy ground, while the trunk is so stunted it can barely be seen. A mere shadow. But then when I look back to where I walked earlier it's like looking down over a coastal inlet once ravaged by the sea.

Later on I ask the question, *Why does it look the way it looks now?* and learn that the wind-blown sand which underlies most of the common is believed to have formed around ten-thousand years ago when Britain was a desert of ice coming out of the last ice age. In this cold tundra strong winds would have blown the sand from exposed river terraces and deposited spreads of it on the flanks of the Stour Valley.

The timpani leads; clarinets, bassoons and French horns follow, until the double basses pick a melody out of the seeming chaos. The melody is pursued, changed, underlined and undermined by other groups of instruments when suddenly the piccolo players and flautists take possession and trip along with it for a while. The double basses take it back, polishing, refining and elaborating upon it, then sharing it with the oboes until I am listening to at least three inter-related yet distinctive melody lines.

As I leave Hartlebury Common the random choice selected by my mysterious music machine is the fourth movement of Beethoven's Ninth. Beethoven, named by Ivan Fischer as 'the composer of the human soul.' The Ninth Symphony. Lauded by Alex and his Droogs in Anthony Burgess' 'A Clockwork Orange,' as the Glorious Ninth.

At breakneck speed in my chariot I fly. The common ragwort of the heath and of my mind now appears on the central reservation. As the Glorious Ninth progresses the daisy-like flowers of this handsome plant swell and grow into bouquets. The outer florets spread from the central disc like the rays of a symbolic sun, twisting and curling and reaching for the sky.

The Ode to Joy begins to build out of the common ragwort and the black and yellow-hooped caterpillars are transformed into numerous chrysalises which, on completion of eclosure, produce in muted brightness, creatures somewhere between scarlet and terracotta. The cinnabar moths take flight and out of the chaos the whole orchestra is in complete harmony. And then the march as the huge ragwort glows gold, freefall portal opens wide, and the music shines 'brighter than a thousand suns'.

The climactic tumult of solo voices and choir ends suddenly in silence and out of that silence the bassoon sets the pace of the martial music. Triangles take over, woodwinds mellow the march, piccolos pipe up, and the tenor sings praise to the 'sonnen fliegen.' The voices of drums enter the fray, the tenor throws the flying suns into the air and they possess the flutes and piccolos. The whole world races until, from under the earth, the depth of the brass overwhelms all.

In flight of fancy my imagination soars with the orchestral sturm und drang, into a calculated recklessness. And the whirligig of flying suns creates a sense of self-abandonment, a gadarene rush, that if I let it, might take me anywhere and everywhere.

> 'Gladly! Just as His suns hurtle
> Through the glorious universe,
> So you, brothers, should run your course,
> Joyfully, like a conquering hero.'

It's still Saturday 11th July and I ask myself where to go following the uplift and the energy spent on the heathland at Hartlebury Common. From the promise of paradise associated with the Daughter of Elysium to the Devil's Spittleful, another area of heathland, this one named after a digging Diablo. My first ever visit to this reserve and a gentle climb through the shade of the Scots pine and up the craggy sandstone knoll, presents me with a view across a mosaic of heathland, grassland, scrub and trees. As I rest in my enervated state I notice the scrub is advancing. A reminder that the heathland requires long-term management and a human input which is notably lacking since lockdown. I know as well that this is part of a group of heathland reserves within the Wyre Forest which have been identified as a priority in Worcestershire's 'Living Landscapes' approach. As these mysterious habitats become increasingly important in fulfilling my need to withdraw I resolve to do anything I can to assist in the alleviation of the threats facing these increasingly rare areas of heathland. Rest and recovery continues as I listen to the distant magic of yellowhammers and skylarks singing, and watch a perky black and tan stonechat on prominent perch, calling and tail-flicking in high dudgeon.

Tuesday 14th July

Always a favourite walk with Dave and I. From Worcester to the Malvern Hills, through the Wyche Cutting, skirt around Ledbury and onto Marcle Ridge to begin.

Blurred into unfocussed presence, from a field of oilseed rape in rain, they declare themselves; two fawns crossing our path. Or perhaps, in the mist that hides and reveals, even fauns?

Heard, not seen, a cuckoo calls as the mists retreat and the kiln pours out memories, and what feels like a hundred sheep, over Woolhope Dome.

Below Marcle Ridge, through seas of grass, two capstans of hay, islands in the sun.

Thursday 16th July

03.30. Another new fox on the block. Black-tipped ears and brush. He dines, walks around the shrubbery. I think I heard him speak: 'Me, no good boyo, up to no good in the wash-house.'

Friday 17th July

I meet Derek on the edge of Sinton Green and take him along a public right of way to Thorngrove, a house which was, from 1810 to 1813, the residence of Lucien Bonaparte, Prince of Canino, younger brother of Napoleon I, when a prisoner of war in this country. It housed him and his wife and six children. One of those children, Charles Lucien Jules Laurent Bonaparte would have been between seven and ten years of age when he was growing up in the Worcestershire countryside. In later life he was to become a renowned French biologist and ornithologist. From Sinton Green to Grimley, which, in 851 was known as Grimanlea, meaning, 'a wood haunted by a ghost or spectre.' A walk along the Severn to Bevere Lock and the island of Bevere, said to have been a resort of beavers. In 1637, during the plague, it was a retreat of the inhabitants of Worcester and in the1870s was a popular bathing-place. Now it's a perfect place for the green woodpecker and the kingfisher. From here to Grimley gravel pits where Derek notices the stunning bright blue flowers and pink stamens of the viper's bugloss and we listen for the calls of the marsh frogs. Another historically noteworthy venue was Monckewood, first recorded in 1240 and owned for centuries by Worcester Priory. Now a nature reserve jointly managed by Worcestershire Wildlife Trust and Butterfly Conservation and known as Monkwood. In the short time we are there speckled wood, comma and white admiral are out in force.

BEING THERE: THE CLENT HILLS

Monday 20th July

A place to embrace. The Clent Hills, Frankley Beeches, Lickey Hills and Bromsgrove. Being there, 'at the still point of the turning world.' Rivers Stour and Arrow running through. From the toposcope I see Kidderminster, Dudley, Birmingham, Droitwich, Stourport, the surrounding urban sprawl. Further out, to north, south, east and west, Abberley Hill, Wolverhampton, Coventry, Warwick, Stratford-on-Avon and Worcester form the flanks. Next in line Evesham, Bredon Hill, Great Malvern, the Malvern Hills, Bromyard Downs and the Clee Hills. Then, for me, the outer reaches. The Cotswold Hills, Cheltenham, Gloucester, May Hill, Leominster, Ludlow, The Long Mynd, The Caradoc Range and the Wrekin. Watling Street, rivers Severn, Teme & Avon, and the M6 weave their way through this tapestry. Stroud & The Forest of Dean the boundaries of my Elysian Lockdown.

One of the first flowers, along with the daisy, the dandelion and the bluebell, that I learned to recognise; another bell, the harebell, its delicate blue bells nodding in the slight breeze. After the toposcope this is the first thing to which I give my full attention on the Clent Hills. Next are man-made objects with which we are so familiar they often escape our notice.

Pylon is the Grecian term for a monumental gateway of an Egyptian temple. While this takes us back to the ancient past, the pylons that cross the Clent Hills were at one time symbols of the future. Placed in a landscape that has been largely unchanged for centuries, they are now familiar in the present. To Stephen Spender, writing in the nineteen-thirties, they had qualities, invasive, alien and mysterious. *The Pylons.*

In amongst hawthorn and holly a solitary goldfinch feeds as I search for landmarks in and beyond the Worcestershire countryside. The Malverns, immediately recognisable, are not far away but what are those blue forgotten hills further in the distance? Storying out of this terrain what do I hear and see up here? A tide of traffic without the moon. Beethoven once again, brought on by a single bouquet of yellow ragwort. 'You are the music while the music lasts.' The uninterrupted sound of grasshoppers, the mystery of the pink flowers growing amongst the golden gorse, more harebells, skylarks; some singing, some hiding where the grass grows in tussocks. A huge basin of trees interlocked by brambles' crochet hooks and the rigid spines of gorse. Puffballs and parasols in troops. The shiny waxcaps of the grasslands. At one point I stand at eye level with so many trees it is kaleidoscopic in its pattern and colour changes but all the more impressive in its easy green repose. Who says it's not easy being green? Well, it was Joe Raposo who wrote it but famously sung by Jim Henson as Kermit the Frog, Frank Sinatra, Ray Charles and Van Morrison. In the Muppet version, Kermit begins with a lament on his greenness. Although he wishes to be some other colour he does not specify but complains that green 'blends in with so many ordinary things.' The denouement is somewhat unexpected, as after his reflections Kermit's associations with the colour green take on a positive hue. In conclusion he asserts himself as a frog of colour, determined to embrace his greenness.

Back on planet earth and back in the purlieus of the Clent Hills the drooping catkins and serrated leaves of the sweet chestnut meld into the darker green leaves of the coppiced hazel which in turn appears to do its utmost to hide the thinly scattered lilac. There's no danger of hiding the handsome ash or the rounded crown and bright green foliage of the walnut, and the beech, I know, stands firm even if from this vantage point I can't see how soundly rooted, firm-footed it is in earth. And the diamond bark of the grey poplar effortlessly draws attention to itself, while the 'aspens dear, whose airy cages quelled or quenched in leaves the leaping sun,' can be heard gently trembling in the growing breeze. Embrace it all.

Early in August Jacky tells me to be very careful when I plant foxgloves, a gift from neighbours Mel and Chris, adjacent to the ox-eye daisies still in bloom, the bird's-foot trefoil and ragged robin. They are poisonous she reminds me. And she's right to do so as the plant is poisonous in every part. Two weeks earlier, on the Clent Hills, I was doing something I had never done before. I have frequently watched fascinated as a bee nudged its way into a foxglove bell, but for the first time I picked one from what could be as many as eighty separate flowers on a single, tall stem. As I couldn't, bee-like, nudge my way in I pinched it between finger and thumb, just as me mam showed me with snapdragons, and, much later, antirrhinum, when I had mastered the pronunciation. Like a shell-pink mouth it opened to me, taking me for a moment to the fig in *Women in Love*. Finger tips touched the glistening velvet and felt fine hairs, diminutive, translucent scales and labial palps, all enclosed in mystery.

The Clent Hills range consists of a number of hills including the Wasely

Hills. The name may come from a combination of waer meaning sheep and ley meaning field or pasture. There doesn't appear to be anything else here, other than the name ley, to suggest that the Clent Hills range constitutes any feature of Alfred Watkins' imagined ley-lines. Not even the four stones on the summit of Clent Hill itself have any claim to such significance, having been placed there on the instruction of Lord Lyttelton of Hagley Hall who also had various other follies, including a Temple of Theseus and a full sized ruined, mock castle constructed on the hills. Although now officially discredited, the concept of ley-lines still has considerable emotional resonance for some and it isn't difficult to feel the significance of Watkins' hypothetical landscape alignment by spending some time studying the toposcope at the summit of Clent Hill and the surrounding terrain itself and letting one's imagination soar.

The yellow tormentil and birdsfoot trefoil gleam golden yellow on the springy slopes and my tormentil thoughts spring from one thing to another. The first time I noticed the neat little four-petalled yellow plant was on St Kilda but I really didn't have to go that far to see it as it is widespread in fens, bogs and heathlands throughout the UK. And although I do recall the significance of tormentil as a herbal remedy it is something else which it always brings to mind. It was a Vanessa who named it for me on St Kilda, and it is the quivering lips and trembling facial expression of Vanessa Redgrave as Ann Boleyn responding to Robert Shaw as Henry VIII singing Lord Randal that appear whenever I see tormentil.

From the yellow tormentil to the blue of germander speedwell and a return to the Isles of Scilly and the sandbar crossing between St Agnes and Gugh where Jan Struther's 'shining sapphires' had spread along the path edges and the grassy plains. From this diversion I return to the Clent Hills and into Segbourne Coppice where the first thing that strikes me about the sky-blue flowers with bright yellow centres, growing next to the pool just off the path to my right, is their texture. Until I edge along the bank to take a closer look they seem waxy, but on closer inspection remind me of the icing-sugar flowers my mother used to make as part of her cake-decorating pursuits in the 1950s. Water forget-me-not (myosotis scorpioides) was once more commonly known as 'scorpion-grass', because its curled clusters resembled a scorpion's tail. The more popular name forget-me-not is a direct translation from the Old French *ne m'oubliez mye*, 'do not forget me.' Renaissance romantics believed that, if they wore these flowers, they would never be forgotten by their lovers, making the flower a symbol of fidelity and everlasting love. This idea was neatly developed by Samuel Taylor Coleridge in *The Keepsake,* where the poet's love Emmeline, knowing that the flowers would fade over time, embroidered,

> 'Between the Moss-Rose and Forget-me-not—
> Her own dear name, with her own auburn hair!'

> So will not fade the flowers which Emmeline
> With delicate fingers on the snow-white silk
> Has worked, (the flowers which most she knew I loved,)
> And, more beloved than they, her auburn hair.'

Wheeze of greenfinch, coo of dove, the buzzing of grasshoppers talking back and forth in rhyme. It has not been very warm for a July day but as I leave the damp and noiseless shade of Segbourne Coppice for the grassy track and banks of a tree-lined rural ride I am transported into summer, quintessential summer. As my pace slows, a grasshopper lands in front of me, silently settles into symmetrical perfection, and begins to stridulate, the long hind legs rubbing against the wings to produce a buzzing, singing sound. And now I'm on a hill top where a wood known as Jubilee Plantation was planted in the mid-seventies to celebrate the Silver Jubilee of Queen Elizabeth II. Many of the trees in this wood are beech to reflect the locally famous Frankley Beeches, a legacy of the Cadbury family, cared for by the National Trust and serving as a visible resistance to the relentless pressure of urbanisation swamping the surrounding area.

This is an experience that I will reprise, but in the spring rather than July, when I can stand, or perhaps sit, and look up into the soothing canopy of green, 'Annihilating all that's made/To a green thought in a green shade.'

Leaving behind the pylons but carrying with me many new connections prompted by walking and watching I make my way back to the car. Fellow folk come to mind when I consider the church tower of two-tone bricks and green cupola and the blocks of flats, designed to look like little boxes. How was lockdown for the inhabitants of such flats I wonder. Fellow feeling follows when I recall Lear coming into contact with the plight of the poor and homeless.

'Poor naked wretches, wheresoe'er you are,

That bide the pelting of this pitiless storm,

How shall your houseless heads and unfed sides,

Your loop'd and window'd raggedness, defend you

From seasons such as these? O, I have ta'en

Too little care of this! Take physic, pomp,

Expose thyself to feel what wretches feel,

That thou mayst shake the superflux to them,

And show the heavens more just.'

WILLIAM SHAKESPEARE

The lived experience that was the Clent Hills sent my thinking in many directions, but principally into the problematic conception of time. In these parlous and uncertain times, more than ever before, I am resolved to withdraw. To withdraw, but engage. In a time where time seems to be disintegrating, to enjoy the cosmos with no differentiation between morning, night and day. Such temporal disintegration occurs in Thomas Mann's narrative in *The Magic Mountain* where Hans Castorp finds shelter during a snowstorm, falls asleep, then dreams that his walking, watching and wondering continues. Mann changes time so that it seems to expand to such an extent that when Castorp awakes he has trouble deciding whether he has time left for his evening meal. The analogy of going on holiday to an unfamiliar place may further illustrate this idea. At first it seems as if there is time to explore and discover the new environment so that the days seem long, but after a few days familiarisation with the place and the routine, time appears to accelerate. This phenomenon can make an experience, such as lockdown, a time where time shrinks rather than expands; time runs so quickly that a month is over before we know it. Just the opposite of course may occur for others. Such are the vicissitudes of time.

SCRIBBLY JACKS AND ALOUETTES: PRESTBURY HILL, CLEEVE COMMON AND CLEEVE HILL

Tuesday 21st July

High on the Cotswold scarp a parking space adjacent to the Bill Smyllie butterfly reserve left me with a short walk, along the hedgerows bordering the lane and beyond the beech plantation, to meet my long-time friend Dave who was parked next to the Masts Field, within the Cleeve Common Site of Special Scientific Interest. As I walk I'm back in the 1950s listening to the yellowhammer's song, usually rendered as 'a little bit of bread and no cheeeeese.' The scribbly Jack as he was known in the North East was also, in other areas of the UK, the writing lark, scribbling lark or scribe. To understand why, consider the eggs. The ground colour of them varies from a dirty white to a pale purplish or brownish tinge. But on this blank page, lines and scribbles of a dark colour range from a deep purplish brown to near black. Sometimes, when Jack has really gone to town, the lines are thicker and spots and blotches are also present.

From the moment we arrived to walk the purlieus of Prestbury Hill the sun shone and the masts gleamed as they reached into the sky-blue sky, dwarfing the shrubs scattered over the common. Vapour trails of the morning flights fading now to leave the sky a sheet of barren blue for the alouettes to fertilise with their song, sheep grazing at the horizon evoking a Biblical feel; the promise of a Fertile Crescent of the Cotswolds. Other than a heat haze coming over the far-reaching common, everything is bright and distinct under the morning light. Thistles, gorse and grass and beyond a tree line, the Cotswold ridge. Biblical seems particularly felicitous a word when suddenly at my feet the tall flower spikes of great mullein, or Aaron's rod, stand staff-like in appearance.

What a change as the common brings us to a local habitation, without a name as far as I can see, but demarcated by a fence along which is a stunning stand of oak and sycamore. Beyond the domes of English oak and French sycamore a row of Lombardy poplars and consolidating this cosmopolitan scene, Pampas grass and golden weeping willow. Following a short rest, a climb confronts us. The words of Nicola Chester in a recent article in the RSPB magazine about walking and wellbeing accompany me on what is a steep ascent. 'Our minds wander' she says, explaining that they are 'responding to sensory stimulants in nature – colours, shapes, smells, movement and sounds.' This is certainly so in my experience, where sometimes such stimulants may take me further into the natural world, or may take me somewhere else, quite outside of it.

Take your time I said to Dave as he started the climb. Take your time Buddy. Then a neat little Buddy Holly song with an apposite refrain arrived on cue.

> 'Take your time, I can wait
> For all the love I know will be mine
> If you take your time
>
> Take your time, though it's late
> Heart strings will sing like a string of twine
> If you take your time
> Take your time and take mine too
> I have time to spend
> Take your time go with me through
> Times 'till all times end
>
> Take your time, I can wait
> For all the love I know will be mine
> If you take your time.'

The song is just short of two minutes. Buddy Holly's life was just too short. And there's something achingly moving in the irony of an inspired young musician singing, 'I have time to spend,' when his time was to come to an abrupt end. Perhaps the young Buddy Holly, like the much older Harold Bloom, combined a love of life with the befriending of death .... 'Take your time go with me through/Times 'till all times end.' Buddy Holly. Died 1959, aged twenty-two. Harold Bloom. Died 2019, aged eighty-nine.

The meadow crane's-bill colours the meadow a vivid violet-blue and the alouettes colour the sky with their warbling song, ascending and descending on a virtually vertical line. A view of the Malverns while we picnic in a lane and the scribbly jacks, nesting on the ground or in the low, dense bushes and the hedge banks bordering the ditches, accompany the alouettes with their high-pitched song, 'a little bit of bread and no cheeeeese.' And in the ditches lady's bedstraw and selfheal rising above the grass of the meadows. Yellow-wort I have only seen once before but I recognize the fused pairs of leaves on the stem. Then the scrambling panicles and perfect, tiny white flowers of hedge bedstraw or galium mollugo, intriguingly translated as false baby's breath.

And as we walk we leave these things, and a road not taken, behind us. And did it make a difference? Well, this is where the other took us, and lichen is what we noticed. It was the colour that Dave pointed out. Quite striking the orangey-yellow on grey. What we might think of as an artist's eye at work. Or perhaps completely natural? The rock crevice home to a family of stoats? Or perhaps a common lizard?

'*Xanthoriaparietina* is a foliose, or leafy, lichen. It has wide distribution, and many common names such as common orange lichen, yellow scale, maritime sunburst lichen and shore lichen. It can be found near the shore on rocks or walls, hence the epithet parietina meaning 'on walls', and also on inland rocks, walls, or tree bark. Often found near farmland and around livestock, the lichen is used as a food source and shelter for the snail *Baleaperversa*.

Xanthoriaparietina is a very pollution-tolerant species. In laboratory experiments, this species can tolerate exposure to air contaminants and bisulphite ions with little or no damaging effect. It is also tolerant of heavy metal contamination. For these reasons, this species has found use as a biomonitor for measuring levels of toxic element.

The water extract of *Xanthoriaparietina* has good antiviral activity *in vitro*, inhibiting the replication of human parainfluenza virus type 2. In the past it was used as a remedy for jaundice because of its yellow colour.'

As Dave and I say farewell from a distance I look down at what feels like a symbol of the inequitable nature of lockdown: the crowded spike of agrimony's starry flowers and then the tall field scabious, its flower heads progressively more divided at the top of the plant.

It's early evening and I'm back at the Bill Smyllie butterfly reserve. As I take my seat, surrounded by lady's bedstraw and rosebay willowherb in abundance I'm reminded that this is the place I saw a Duke of Burgundy butterfly a couple of years ago but this is the wrong time of year for a repeat. And so I sit, and wait and see. And what I see is something which appears to be watching me. I lean forward a little but am immediately detected and the observer scurries back into what appears to be a den. I learn later that this is a mesh-web spider. The female builds a web on the ground to catch prey such as beetles and other crawling insects. According to one of the few references I can find to these creatures 'the male drums on the web to announce he is calling.' What he may be calling for is not revealed.

Looking beyond the small yellow clusters of lady's bedstraw and the tall stems of the rosebay willowherb bright with purple flowers, I notice the lilac flowerheads of field scabious nodding in the gentle breeze. As I feel myself nodding too I decide to take a stroll. Almost every step is a revelation. The quaking grass, about which I read on the reserve signboard, is trembling in the light breeze. It also makes a rattling sound not far removed from the popping seedpods which were one of the many musics of Hartlebury Common. This attractive feature of the trembling, rattling grass is followed by the delightful sight of honey-bees on the pink carpet of wild thyme and the spikes of viper's-bugloss with its stunning blue flowers. Then the butterflies put in an appearance. The leaves of the stunted hawthorn are green but the berries are smudged with yellow ochre and when a meadow brown alights on the bush the splash of orange around the eyespot blends in beautifully. Within seconds I have a chance to compare the small heath which lands on the nearby field scabious. It is really *very* small; a meadow brown in miniature. And then what turns out to be the last butterfly of the day. Chocolate-brown with a band of orange half-moons on the wing edges. Brown argus. 'Beauty truly blent.'

I return to my seat and look across to Prestbury Park and Cheltenham race course, letting my eyes run toward the horizon and along the Cotswold ridge. Scanning the familiar terrain the quality of the light makes it easy to pick out Hay Bluff and May Hill in the far distance, then Bredon Hill close by. And closer still, the Malvern Hills.

'In a somer seson
Whan softe was the sonne,
As on a May morwenynge
On Malverne hilles
I was wery for-wandred
And wente me to reste
Under a brood bank
By a bournessyde;
And as I lay and lenede
And loked on the watres,
I slombred into a slepyng
That I was in a wildernesse,
A depe dale bynethe,
With depe diches and derke.
A fair feeldful of folk
Fond I ther bitwene
Of alle manere of men,
The meene and the riche,
Werchynge and wandrynge
As the world asketh.'

Not my dream but the opening to a picture of life in the 14th century, written by William Langland. 'The field full of folk' and 'all manner of men,' 'working and wandering,' resonated with thoughts of the 2020 Cheltenham Festival.

I can't say what makes me look down but there he is, a dainty little lizard. The common lizard is prey to many animals; the kestrel accounts for most, but other birds and rats and snakes present a further threat. Perhaps this is a reason for the common lizard being yet another creature in decline. But then there's habitat loss. Loss of open woodland, loss of heathland, loss of moorland and loss of gardens. So that accounts for the human contribution.

The afternoon heat had stilled the gentle breeze and now all was still, though not the scribbly jacks and the alouettes who still would not be stilled.

COLOURS: THE PURLIEUS OF GRIMLEY GRAVEL PITS

Thursday 30th July

Brown, black, blue, buff, chestnut, chocolate-brown, cream, creamy-yellow, dark brown, dark green, golden-brown, green-blue, greenish yellow, grey, grey-brown, orange, orange-red, pale brown, pale grey, pink, reddish orange, wax-red, white and yellow. Every colour under the sun, including sky blue pink with a finny addy border and the horse of a different colour. First was a speckled wood, blurred brown and cream in green shade. Blue on stone-cold stone, short-bodied chaser followed. Gatekeeper next, whose path I crossed after his stunning orange-in-sunlight upperside halted me, and his double-pupiled eyespots held me in his gaze. Two common terns but uncommon colours; grey some may say, French grey I say, only really matched by the handsome wheatear in his summer plumage. Then the calls of these common terns painted on the air with measured beats, up and down in black and white. Forked tail of white, black crown and nape, vermilion bill the apogee.

A lapwing flock in flight fairly slow, the pace of the adagietto from Mahler's 5th, as if shot through a window on the sky to give depth in contrast to a few jaded birds on the foregrounding shore. Four little egrets enter the picture, pure white elegance stabbing for fish in point counterpoint chords. Crimson bills and chocolate brown heads of black-headed gulls, silver-grey mantles and wings tipped with black, sharing the shoreline with a scattering of starlings. I count three, all iridescent green and purple under the summer sun, until I notice the subtle white spotting on the breast. It's then that the dabchick's whinnying call alerts me to his chestnut neck and cheeks, but soon leaves me looking at waves radiating out from where he neatly dives. Three geese sail sedately into view, barred grey-brown backs and white rumps in common. Two with white cheeks, black heads and necks, the other orange billed, tip dipped in white. Two Canada, one greylag. A small colony of herring gulls, the mottled grey-brown of these immature birds quite some way off the pure white and silver-grey mantle and wings of the adult plumage. Over the next three years the dull pink legs will brighten and the dark bill will become a striking yellow with an orange spot near the tip. Three oystercatchers keep out of the way but their noisy piping and bold black and wite colouration is difficult to conceal. And impossible to miss the long, orange-red bill, pink legs and red eyes.

And the cormorants in trees and in rows on fence posts in water, wings out to dry. They appear all black with white patches on face and on thigh, but closer inspection reveals bronze-green wings and tail and blue-black head, neck and underparts. The pair of great crested grebe, a species which were almost wiped out in Britain in the nineteenth century, reveal, even without close inspection, the black cap and twin-horned crest, and the chestnut frills around the long white neck and bordering the pale cheeks. These feathers graced other long white necks and heads when grebe feathers became a fashion item. Reflecting on the protection now afforded to these birds, and on the elaborate courtship display I experienced earlier in the year, I begin to wonder why I'm not seeing the familiar, familial picture of the young being carried on the backs of the parent birds. My thoughts of the black and white humbug-striped heads of the young birds take flight, as a small tortoiseshell butterfly alights on the reddish-purple florets of the black knapweed at my feet. Brightly speckled orange and black wings. Blue crescents create a margin on a black band along the outside edges of all four wings. A meadow brown, a small white and a large white enter the scene to add dark brown with a splash of orange, black, white and pale yellow with a dusting of grey scales to this palette of natural colours.

Now comes the segue from July into August. August. Venerable like Bede, Hallowed as the Name of God. And the symbol for August, its birth flower, the gladiolus or poppy, meaning beauty, strength of character and love, and associated with marriage and the family.

The second day of August and a walk just beyond Grimley gravel pits, along the River Severn, through a wood and into the sheep and horse pastures. From the hedgerow-filled fencing surrounding the pastures a familiar call, the loud 'hooeet' of redstarts on passage. A small family in amongst the hawthorn and elder. One striking male, chestnut tail, rump and underparts that give him his name –*steort* the Old English for tail – complemented by a white forehead, black throat and grey mantle. Along with three other birds, one a female with a pale orange wash and the other two, grey-brown juveniles, fluttering in and out of the foliage and picking up food from the ground. It's something of a contrast when I arrive at

Grimley gravel pits to see six little egrets, long head-plumes adorning all-white plumage, black, dagger-like bill and black legs with bright yellow feet. Two resting in an alder, two standing motionless in the reeds, the remaining two feeding energetically, in pursuit of prey with stabbing bills.

CARAVAGGIO AND THE BROWN HAIRSTREAK: GRAFTON WOOD

Monday 3rd August

St John the Baptist Church near Grafton Flyford, Worcestershire, is a Grade II, listed building. The church car park provides access to the ancient woodland of Grafton Wood, once a part of the medieval Royal Forest of Feckenham. After a ten-minute walk along a footpath, through a farmyard and over open fields, I pass through the kissing gate into the wood. Appropriately enough the butterfly in attendance is a gatekeeper. Walking along a woodland ride, sun-graced glades amongst the lofty ash and the oak's spreading crown, warm buzzing and chirping sounds vibrating in my ears, I am in a dream-space. In quick succession, crossing and re-crossing my chosen path, three butterflies pursue their erratic, fluttering, flight pattern, the familiar meadow brown and velvety speckled wood, and slow and low in delicate flight, the scarcer wood white. Next comes the brimstone, employing the technique of swimming through the air in a figure of eight pattern to ensure safety from predators. This safety is further ensured by the distinctive leaf-shaped wings, providing effective camouflage during rests between short flight periods. Watching these fluctuating patterns of flight, coupled with the increasing warmth, and bombardment of sound, is a pleasant but dizzying assault to the senses, so I am pleased to have brought a seat with me. I choose a place to place my seat. A place in the shade. On the edge of a copse of sapling blackthorn, scrub and shrub, of field maple, hawthorn and hazel, at the conjunction of three paths. This turns out to be something of a place of magic visions. Brimstones at first, still dizzying me even as I sit. A flying flame of blazing orange along the ride and soon I am mesmerised by the playing of the silver-washed fritillaries; chasing one another across the sunny clearings then resting on leaves or the dead and decaying wood intentionally left to help this habitat thrive. The pace is slowed to a dream as a red admiral drinks from a puddle, a small white flies into sight and I am on my way to another island now. From Grafton Flyford in soporific flight I fly. To an island of dreams. To Malta. To another St John's church. St John's Co-Cathedral in the capital city, Valletta. Day and night, stair-rod rain. Darkness dominating the capital. And yet there was a beam of light in the darkness, the mysterious gloom of Michelangelo Merisi da Caravaggio's chiaroscuro discernible. Every other feature engulfed in shadows flat and unfathomable. But for the corner where I sit and where I dream. A corner rich in darkness and light. There the warm yellow of the brimstone butterfly and vivid scarlet of the red admiral. There the Oratory. A small chapel for private worship. The chapel dominated by a painting depicting The Beheading of St John the Baptist in Caravaggio's Baroque palette. Verdigris, vermilion, red ochre, umber. Rich in light, richer in darkness. Yellow, white and carbon black. A circle of light illuminating the scene of the beheading. A painting both sacred and real. Sallow, yellow flesh of perpetrator and witnesses, the buttery brimstone, and the red cape draped around St John, an unintended echo of the diagonal stripes on the red admiral's wings. And then the detail of the trickle of blood from the neck of St John, spreading on the ground to form the signature of Caravaggio. A symbolic seal in blood, and perhaps a reminder of the blood Caravaggio spilled in the brawl that brought him to Valletta.

Even in the act of writing as the dream is re-imagined, the music floats in. A violin concerto in full Baroque fruition. Bach's Concerto for violin, strings and continuo in E major. The first movement is an allegro, and is what Jacky is listening to as I depart my Baroque dream and return to reality. And the reality with which I am confronted is something which never fails to stun me. The largest wingspan of any British dragonfly. And fast. This is the emperor dragonfly, hawking its territory for prey. It settles for some time, allowing me to study its huge eyes, its brilliant blue abdomen, banded black, and green thorax, until a peacock butterfly happens by and the emperor is in pursuit.

I pause to look down at the gold-centred and yellow-petalled flower at my feet. This is a flower that always strikes me as a particularly neat version of the ragged common ragwort. This is common fleabane, named after the belief that when the plant was burnt the smoke would drive away fleas. Remarkably, every single flower-head of this daisy-like flower has packed into it around six-hundred florets. A small skipper, speeding and darting in the vicinity creates a corner of a lost world in miniature, coming down to land on the six-hundred florets, its hind-wings slightly backwards like a swing-wing. I'm almost back to the kissing gate, the point of departure from the wood, walking by the wild angelica with its umbrellas of flowers and stems covered in downy hairs. But there's something on the angelica. Something basking in the late afternoon sun. Rich brown above, coppery orange beneath. Two small, distinctive tails and two wavy white streaks on the underside. This is a creature I have never seen before. One who I know feeds on aphid honeydew. I stand in this precious moment and remembered words cut in:

> 'Weave a circle round him thrice,
> And close your eyes with holy dread,
> For he on honey-dew hath fed,
> And drunk the milk of Paradise.'

And what was by turns a dream-space, a place of magic visions, and a lost world, is now a rural idyll with a brown hairstreak butterfly to see me out as the gatekeeper saw me in.

LANDFILL THRILL: THROCKMORTON

Monday 10th August

In shafts of sunlight sparkling through the canopy of oak and sycamore, a speckled wood butterfly dances in lively flight. At a much more measured pace, I make my way toward the large pool, taking full advantage of the woodland shade, until suddenly I'm there, in a place of surprising serenity. The torrid heat mutes the sounds of ducks and finches and even the gulls flying off in fright at my appearance barely disturb the tranquility. I set up my trusty chair, adjust my hat to achieve maximum protection against the sun and survey this scene in solitude. On sandy shore under my feet, printed on this temporary page, tracks and traces, iconic fonts in strange calligraphy of others making their paths through life. Lifting my eyes up to see something of the bigger picture I think to myself I have never seen teasel in such abundance. The growth on the edge of the pool directly in front of me is prolific, towering and spreading into a dense mass of leaves and prickly stems with spiny, oval heads. It's easy to see why teasel is considered to be an invasive species in the United States, liable to crowd out all native plants and form a monoculture. Scanning the further reaches of the pool edge I notice the teasel thinning out, and, mingling with the water mint, the golden-plumed, brown, velvety sausages of bulrushes and the solitary, rosy flowers of great willowherb, inviting me to walk into the marshy terrain ahead. Stretching up the bank behind me the craqueleure of earth's crust is like parched crazy paving. This craqueleure, unlike the Murillo painting I admired in the Church of the Holy Spirit on the Isle of Wight, is of earth's drying crust and reads to me like a warning. Not the San Andreas fault, but this miniaturised equivalent is a mélange of fractures and cracks and sagging pieces of the earth's surface. So, not the way to go I decide.

As the leaves of the water mint are crushed underfoot and the pungent smell perfumes the air, the walk into the teasels, bulrushes, willowherb and water mint turns out to be stimulating not only to the sense of sight. Under the blinding luminance of the sun the little egrets and mute swans shine dazzlingly white, and the didappers redouble their dives as a solitary swift flies over. I follow it as it skims across the surface of the pool, the pool almost identical in its hue to the azure sky. My eyes fall on a sizeable congregation of Canada geese and coots, and in amongst them a pair of tufted ducks, an extended family of ducklings in their care. Herring gulls and lesser black-backed gulls are also present in numbers but un-characteristically even they are silent and calm under the sapping heat of the midday sun.

Libellula depressa. Maybe it's just the sun getting to me but the sonorous sound of the Latin name seems perfect for the broad-bodied chaser with its flattened, blue abdomen, frosted like a sloe berry. I watch this dragonfly flying swiftly along the margins of the pond and returning predictably to the same low perch, or occasionally varying it by landing on some dry, exposed stones and positioning himself carefully to take full advantage of the solar energy. This is also the ideal habitat for the common blue damselfly and it does not disappoint. Vividly enamelled in pale blue and black hoops, it is notable enough when at rest, or when in massive flight well out over the water, but probably at its most impressive when, during mating, the male clasps the female by her neck while she bends her body around to his reproductive organs in what is described as 'the mating wheel.'

'Insatiate' is the epithet Shakespeare chose to characterise the prodigious greed of the cormorant and it comes to mind in this moment as I watch a group of these birds on a stony promontory, just visible through the thinned-out teasels. While not really fair to the bird, which crams its crop full of fish in order to feed its young through regurgitation, it is a salutary reminder of the human exploitation of animals. Since the sixth century cormorants have been used, particularly in Japan and China, to catch fish by the simple, but cruel, technique of tying a snare near the base of the bird's throat. Once a traditional means of human sustenance, cormorant fishing, as it is known, is now more of a tourist attraction. A solitary tourist, I watch this group of five, stock-still on the end of the promontory, bills open rather than wings, and not for food but to help them to cool down. Taking my cue from the cormorants I decide to walk round to the other side of the pool and, avoiding the prohibited landfill operations area I find a shaded avenue through the osier and grey willow, along the waterside. The osiers here have not been coppiced so the long and narrow, green and silver leaves afford protection from the sun, which is not only effective but also attractive. The grey willows as well offer me dual benefits – the attraction of their fissured grey-brown bark and silvery-grey felted leaves, together with the cool cloister of dense foliage. For a moment I stand in a clearing, from which I venture into, and immediately out of, a thicket of rampant bramble and blackthorn. Relieved to be out of this reminder of a place, more Golgotha or Gesthemane than Eden or Avalon, I take a detour in the other direction to reach two smaller pools, which proved difficult to access for the marshy ground surrounding them. Keen to avoid this potential Slough of Despond I make my road by walking in another direction. In the short time since I failed to reach the two pools I had removed my shirt and my vest was now sticking to my body. Picking my way toward the large pool I peer at the trees in front of me with screwed up eyes to combat the dazzling sunlight. I walk in darkness for a moment, opening my eyes to an abandoned orchard. A bounteous collection of apples and pears. Most of the trees in fruit, though not yet ripe. Redcurrants, delighting in the scientific name, *ribes rubrum*, translucent and glistening; elderberry clusters, lustrous blue-black pearls. A paradise garden next to the pool. The tansy flowerheads, golden buttons flashing in the sun. Common fleabane, the ubiquitous tormentil and the common ragwort ringing with some remembered resonance of the same yellow colour scheme back on the Isle of Wight. Birds foot trefoil adds to the singular colour riot.

In prone position, I watch a common blue butterfly, the last of the meadow browns and bees galore. Tree bumblebees in their ginger, black and white-hooped rugby shirts. White-tailed bumblebees on field scabious. Common carder bees on the gorse. *Libellula depressa*. Those sun-induced words once more. A broad-bodied chaser. This time a female, splendid golden-brown under the searing, summer sun. Reddish hue and pale of rump disappearing into wood of oak and sycamore; a deer as I depart. In shafts of sunlight sparkling a speckled wood butterfly dances in lively flight. 'In my end is my beginning.'

SOLITARY SOJOURN: UPPER HOLLOWFIELDS FARM

Thursday 20th August

I arrive at an unknown place, empty of people. East Coker ten days ago. Today, The Waste Land, 'dry sterile thunder without rain' and the heat screams as I step out of the car.

The ground is baked dry and stony underfoot. A painted lady suddenly fills the emptiness and illuminates this mute and impassive ancient field, where it's not difficult to imagine the bare-footed children whose winter task it would have been to clear the fields of stones, stooping and crawling, hands numbing and chilling. What a shaming image in contrast to the tranquility and splendid isolation that is these endless, arable fields. Many arable fields are large and featureless monocultures devoid of wildlife, but this is a place managed sympathetically to benefit wildlife. Wild bird seed mixes are sown, hedges are managed on rotation to cater for the differing requirements of species, including the rare brown hairstreak butterfly. There is an inescapable feeling that the coronavirus has halted much of this as it was just getting underway. And yet. Nature still strives.

The painted lady is still painting the colours of my mind in a delicate pale orange, dotted with black and smudged with white, when there's a sudden rush of meadow brown on the wing. In addition a few speckled wood have opted for the open, sun-drenched meadow rather than the shafts of sunlight in an oak wood with which I tend to associate them. As I continue to walk along the field-edge I notice that both large and small whites have congregated in an exceedingly warm and bright corner which proves to be as compelling and as disorienting as Bridget Riley's 1961 painting, Movement in Squares. Head spinning from a combination of jinking butterflies and seething heat I walk on until I am stopped by the need to sneeze. The ACHOO has the volume of a small explosion and during the eye-closing moment of the sneeze a young roe deer springs out in front of me. My eyes open to this young buck's antlers and foxy-red summer coat but the fluffed out white rump betrays the creature's alarm at my gunshot sneeze. Front and back legs, to stretch entire fully extended, and he's gone.

In the quiet of the roe deer's wake a painted lady fills the emptiness once more. But this time echoing rather than illuminating the muted surroundings. I take the opportunity of looking closely at the detail on the underside wings of this butterfly which will have journeyed from North Africa or the Mediterranean coast of France to be here. The delicately webbed, lace patterning is a subtle and intricate filigree of threads, as subdued as the upperside is bright.

Under the high cloud the sun is now hazy and the heat less oppressive. There is, however, an eerie absence of birds. With that thought some consolation comes when I see something ahead of me on the path. Forewings folded back to conceal hindwings, the magpie moth reveals itself as having been the creation of a budding young artist. First the visible wings have been given a flat wash to produce an even layer of white. Next the body and the tops of the wings near the head, and a line from one wing-edge to the other, have been coloured golden-yellow. A final touch is a formal neatness, consolidated by the application of black dots in gently waving lines along the edges of the wings and across the body.

Suddenly I'm in the company of two roe deer. The doe, appreciably smaller than the buck, and without antlers, intuits the shortest distance between two points and since it's an open field a glorious view is on offer as she races away from me. I take up the offer, noticing how relaxed and rangy this creature is as she bounces and leaps through a space of her own. The other is in clover but not in the human sense of luxuriating. Having spotted me, what appeared a place of easy eating of fresh shoots and over-hanging branches of deciduous trees, or a place to rest in the heather and warm grass, has now become a snare of tangled brambles and tall clover. His nerves, and mine, jangle as his freedom is threatened by my presence. I freeze at the sight of terror in his eyes. I back off. In reckless haste he's unensnared. He's flying.

In the boundless hedges of blackthorn, sloe berries jet black under the cloudy bloom. This is late summer. The time for the female brown hairstreak to lay eggs in the forks of the blackthorn.

From Lesser Stitchwort to Autumn Lady's Tresses: Hollybed Farm Meadows and Castlemorton Common

Friday 21st August

On Far Starling Bank the meadow vetchling scrambles and climbs over the grassland, as if aware of its beneficial effect on the meadows it inhabits. In the past this scrambling plant would have been encouraged by farmers, because its roots increase the richness of the soil by drawing nitrogen from the air. In addition, the fact that the plant is also rich in protein, adds to the food value of pasturage and hay. It is these factors, as well as being a host to the wood white butterfly, which make meadow vetchling one of the keys to the vision of a 'Living Landscape'.

Hogweed decorates and dominates the verges next to the trees, but with a predilection for the perfection in what is miniscule, the dainty white flowers of the lesser stitchwort are the cynosure of my eyes. It is some time since the great willowherb commandeered the field-side ditch for itself, so although it still shows, the once bright flowers are now fading patches of colour. A real surprise is the ragged robin. For a flower of May and June it is well past the end of its season but its long, finger-lobed, delicate petals are still recognizable in this month of August.

Probably the most colourful moment of this walk is provided by a common blue butterfly alighting next to us on some common fleabane and opening and closing its wings in a display that was anything but common. A row of orange spots along the edge of the hindwing and spilling over onto the forewing, together with a neat patterning of white spots with black centres, is repeatedly alternated with a moment of iridescent blue, fringed in white. We are captivated.

Although it's late in the year to experience the full glory of these flower-rich meadows there is still much to appreciate, as I am reminded when Margaret tells me about the most common types of buttercup. The creeping buttercup is the one that spreads rapidly with the help of its overground stolons, or runners. I immediately recognise Margaret's description as the rampant invaders we have in our garden. Meadow buttercup is a rather more majestic buttercup of meadows and hedgerows and other grassy places, and then there's the bulbous buttercup, a plant of shorter grasslands, such as pastures and calcareous grasslands. But the one that really catches my imagination is the goldilocks buttercup. One of the many traditional hay meadow plants that make Far Starling Meadow a Site of Special Scientific Interest. A good reason to return in May or June.

Another familiar yellow flower, wood avens, is one of the successes of my wilding back home. Also known as herb bennet this is a plant of damp, shady places, associated with St Benedict and used in the fifteenth century to ward off evil spirits. Leaving this plant to its Christian duty we move along the edge of the meadow into a waterlogged, wooded terrain, dominated by shrubs rather than trees. It is here that Margaret points out silverweed, its silvery, silky-hairy leaves forming a mat spread by overground stolons. This is an unusual habitat and one where a natural process of succession will lead to wetlands and marshes eventually becoming wet woodland. This state of flux may eventually see a further drying out, and the willow and alder succeeded by broadleaved trees such as oak. But for the present it feels to me that, with the fallen, moss-covered willows dotting the landscape, we have entered the woodland world of an Arthur Rackham illustration, where gnarled and twisted roots and branches conceal elves and goblins, and fairy rings appear in the wood where fairies have 'danced their ringlets to the whistling wind'.

This is a habitat ravaged by man and by weather, where speckled woods are in the wood in mixed-up-confusion of seasons; where sense of smell is startled by herb Robert stench; where pungent water-mint perfumes the air; where darkness of woods leads to light, enchanter's nightshade in shady place; where in depth and density trees and shrubs compose themselves in patterns of light; where speckled yellow moth and red bartsia commune; where great oaks from little acorns grow; where the ash carries the keys; where Jack Orion curses 'oak and ash and bitter thorn;' where winter is on its way; where Shelley shouts 'if winter comes, can spring be far behind?' and Bert Jansch sings of 'springtime promises;' where fleabane and wild angelica thrive.

We're out of the woods. In a place where the wind sings a different tune. Now it's blackberries, hawthorn and brambles. But for a surprise appearance of scattered hay bales, and pastoral of trembling aspen, silver underwings to the leaves; convolvulus pink and white and an ivy-clad cottage, complete the quintessential English picture.

At Damson Tree Lodge a rooster crows as we depart, loaded with Marjorie's seedling plums, damson jam and honey. Slowly past black-faced sheep and onto the common in search of spirals.

A short walk yields up lady's bedstraw, yarrow and tormentil, before Margaret finds the first of two *spiranthes spiralis*. I find the second, my first wild August orchid, autumn lady's tresses, flowers set spirally up the stem.

Wednesday 26th August

Perry Green on Glover's Needle.

Wednesday 2nd September

A return with Dave to one of our old haunts, beginning and ending in Mamble. After the freedom and tranquility of the extensive open fields a change of habitat as we enter Wissett's Wood. Over to Shakenhurst Manor, granted in 1349 by Edward III to his vassal John de Meysey, 'for services rendered overseas,' now a £16 million shooting and trout-fishing estate. Thence over the dismantled Tenbury and Bewdley Railway and across the River Rea to Reaside Manor Farm, adjacent to the magical sounding village of Nineveh, named after the ancient Assyrian city of Upper Mesopotamia, and just south of Cleobury Mortimer. Pausing to appreciate the late 16th to early 17th century manor house with plain old-tiled roof, and projecting rubble stone stacks on each side and at the rear, with diagonal brick shafts with spurs and caps, I recalled how perfect this was for the nesting kestrels we had watched five years ago. I wondered whether kestrels were still utilising this perfect facility and was assured by the lady of the manor that indeed they were. On to Bayton after a picnic in the drizzle, returning full circle to Mamble, but only after pausing to enjoy Jan Struther's speedwell blue and Baroness Orczy's scarlet pimpernel, accompanied by the pineapple weed. The latter I crush to savour the aroma of pineapple.

THE UNMASKED AND THE MASKED: SUTTON PARK

Thursday 3rd September

'Huzzah! What a bird!' I had never been to Sutton Park before this visit but will definitely return. To begin with I did a general reccy in which I walked along Westwood Coppice from Banners Gate, where I was parked. The silver birch foregrounded by the purple heather and golden gorse made for an inviting setting as the showers faded and the sun slowly came through. I then took what turned out to be a circuitous route to Rowton's Well in search of the area which two experienced Worcester birders, Mike and Brian, had indicated as the place in which the bird had been seen. Rowton's Well is an ancient spring of clear water which also turns out to be a medicinal pool with a circular curb of large stones. Although not easy to find, the search for the well helped me familiarise myself with the area, which also included an advantageous elevation, from a tumulus of earth and stones.

Beginnings and endings coincide and collide as I walk through the dying and reviving broom; the purplish sheen of the pods has faded but the disintegrating carapaces remind me of the cracking and bursting seed pods of spring. Into a sea of alternating heather and gorse, and my eye is drawn over wave after wave, until the heather reaches the stand of silver birch, concealing and revealing the vista beyond. Nature aping Capability Brown's aping of nature through his technique of integrating a garden with the landscape beyond. A startled jay, in turn startling me, as it speeds over the dense, high-standing gorse, a blur of pink, brown, blue, white and black.

As long as I don't count the time from the 1950s, when cousin John and I would dream of one day seeing a red-backed shrike, it didn't keep me waiting long. Arriving in undulating flight, it was soon moving from the gorse to crab apple trees, occasionally hovering, then dropping to the ground or into brambles in search of food. He also sat stock-still for some of the time, which pleased the photographers. As there were only seven of them, this helped to make it a tranquil sighting for everyone, and my first ever, of the 'butcher bird,' so-called because of its habit of impaling its prey on thorns and spikes. Time stretched in this serene setting, enabling a thorough appreciation of this bird of rufous-brown back, blue-grey cap, creamy white underparts and a black mask across the eyes. This masked figure, for now a loner among the unmasked.

Indian Summer

Saturday 12th September

Agrimony is the first plant I notice after the descent to the disused railway line at Brotheridge Green which is now a wildlife corridor. What once were embankments are now covered in grass, scrub and saplings, providing a haven for butterflies and birds. I can only walk one way, as under the road bridge the railway cutting is choked with overhanging trees. Before taking the path I reflect on the re-wilding of this once lively, clattering, man-made intrusion, now a tranquil habitat, re-colonised by the natural world. The slender, crowded spike of delicate, star-shaped, yellow flowers which is the agrimony, was believed, in pagan times, to have magical properties. Certainly, it reminds me of a magic wand, and I know that today its coarsely toothed leaflets are still used as a stimulating alternative to tea.

As I walk the only path possible, the two tracks where the railway lines once were, whether I look forwards or backwards, slide together in the distance, reminding me of Eliot's words in the third stanza of Dry Salvages, the third part of Four Quartets:

> 'You shall not think 'the past is finished'
> Or 'the future is before us'.

As I stand in the welcome warmth of an Indian Summer, in these parlous times, in the lived moment of the present, I realise in that moment, that Eliot has already answered the question of time's conundrum in the first stanza of Burnt Norton, the first part of Four Quartets:

> 'Time past and time future
> What might have been and what has been
> Point to one end, which is always present.'

It's too late in the season for the marbled white and white-letter hairstreak but the red admiral, small tortoiseshell and brimstone are around, as well as the last of the meadow browns. Butter-and-eggs, or yellow toadflax, is widespread in this ruderal spot, or where land has been disturbed by human construction. The etymology of the word rubble, from the Latin, rudus, is easy to appreciate as one walks on the ballast of ash, clinker and gravel, still present years after the sleepers and railway lines disappeared. As I walk clear of the embankment and the trees thin out, and in twists and turns reach up to the light, the ash, clinker and gravel corridor is transformed into an obstacle course of hillocks and hummocks, bared tree-roots, spoil-heaps and tunnel entrances. Now it's a colony of badger setts.

Sunday 13th September

The culmination of my previous visit to Grafton Wood was the gift of a brown hairstreak. The cloudless sky under which I walk on this visit is a muted pastel blue, the perfect wash for an arguably, still life study of a left-leaning and decaying oak, hollow in trunk and branches, foregrounded by shadows, and all around a carefully-careless scattering of newly baled hay over short stiff, stalks of stubble. In the background a bed of quickset, interspersed with verdant vegetation.

The 'sun-graced glades' and 'sunny clearings' that defined my first visit to Grafton Wood are replaced by an overwhelming presence of light. At the end of every figurative or literal tunnel, light shines. As Leonard Cohen would have it:

> 'There is a crack, a crack in everything,
> That's how the light gets in.'

There is a striking affinity with TS Eliot in the starting point of the song:

> 'Don't dwell on what has passed away,
> Or what is yet to be.'

Monday 14th September

As on my first visit The Devil's Spittleful serves well as a place of rest and recovery. I sit in my chair amongst the gorse, the broom, the heather and the silver birch. Sounds stifled in the heat of this Indian summer I watch two small copper butterflies and two red admirals and notice autumn leaves on some of the trees. A distinctive ticking sound; flashes of pink, black and white; strings of birds flying from tree to tree. An extended family of long-tailed tits, 'bumbarrels' as John Clare called them. Returning home to Worcester in the luxury of an air-conditioned car I open the doors and step into 26 degrees Celsius and it's 18.45.

Tuesday 15th September

An insect catching congregation over the Severn. Watching the low-level, easy gliding flight of the white-rumped house martins in this very late summer, now I see the golden button-like flowers of tansy and memories of my recklessness with the Fairy Liquid return.

Thursday 17th September

A morning visit to the Old Hills, with Derek and I paying heed to the advice of Richard Thompson (*Keep Your Distance*) and the Police (*Don't Stand So Close To Me*). Much of the time is spent discussing finger-picking, from Mississippi John Hurt to Sara Louise, but still time to notice the speckled woods. And an especially big day as Jacky starts her singing lessons again this afternoon. Hallelujah!

Sunday 20th September

The temperature when I left home around 18.00 was 23 degrees Celsius. I arrived at Grimley to discover many starlings and pied wagtails readying themselves for their roost, along with one hundred plus Canada geese. I walked slowly across the causeway by the Hippo pool and watched the cormorants settling in the big dead alder where I have only seen one hobby this year. Idly I counted them as they seemed to fill the tree. Twenty-two of them, plus two little egrets. Then I noticed the two other dead alders behind them were thick-black with cormorants. Twenty-four in the second. Thirty-four in the third. That amounted to a lot of cormorants. It felt like a worthwhile visitation with so many birds so I decided to do the full circuit, along the edge of the wood, towards the Camp House Inn, then back along the open meadow and over the otter causeway. Arrived at a point where I could see the twenty-two cormorants and two little egrets from a different perspective than the earlier viewing.

That's a big little egret I muttered to myself, as I watched a heron-sized white bird stalking the shallows across the pool. The yellow bill told me. A great white egret. The last one I saw here was around eight years ago.

145

At The Gravel Pits

Moments which choose us,
like that impression of silence
recalled as the great white egret,
an exile in his own kingdom,
walked on the water; this his station
where homage is paid,
here he walks on black, stilted legs.

Awkwardly lordly in the trees,
but see how he ascends brightly,
broadening and silencing the big sky,
span of wings and stillness of flight
flowing through parabolas of grace.

Believe the broad wings that brought him,
an impression of silence, feathering air
as he appears to fill the sky, at last
descending to walk among the multitude;
I only saw the angel afterwards.

INTO AUTUMN

Tuesday 22nd September

A familiar muted and tranquil opening, to a tune of which I never tire, lulls
me along the outskirts of Worcester, past the turning to Elgar's birthplace
in Lower Broadheath. Led by the beautiful melody through the hamlet of
Hallow, along Moseley Road to Monkwood Nature Reserve, Elgar's
Nimrod gently soars and swells to its climax, exercising restraint and
control, throughout its undulating theme and simple variation, all the way
to its dignified close. The car is parked, I'm ready to roam, but not once
I'm mesmerised by the next randomly selected piece. The piece, Dance
No. 3, by Philip Glass, is, like Ravel's Bolero, ostinato based, its rhythms
and melodies relentlessly repeated, but with a stripped-back, churning,
existential essence.

Eighteen minutes and thirty-five seconds later I step out of the car. Birds and butterflies are notable by their absence, but as I traverse the familiar rides I arrive in one corner where the Indian summer of recent days has been supplanted by autumn. Here I find fly agaric fungus in profusion. Some at different stages, their rounded caps still covered with the felty, cream-coloured veil, but most a glorious scarlet, with small patches of the torn veil decorating the crown. These were amongst the birches, but under the beech and oak, capped in deep, reddish-brown, spindle-shanks sprouted, in large tufts, at the foot of trees.

Reflecting on these thriving communities of fungi, and with the existential essence of repeated melodies and rhythms still dancing through me, I drift into thoughts prompted by my recent reading of Robert Macfarlane's *Underland*.

'For centuries, fungi had generally been considered harmful to plants; parasites that caused disease and dysfunction.' Following the research of Suzanne Simard, such long-held conceptions about forest ecosystems were overturned. The importance of a mutual, symbiotic association between a fungus and a plant or what Simard termed 'an underground social network' of fungal threads, linking nearly every tree in a forest, including trees of different species, has now been established. Sometimes referred to as the *wood wide web*, this is a *network of astonishing complexity and extent,* a network in which, 'Instead of seeing trees as individual agents competing for resources, she proposed the forest as a 'co-operative system', in which trees 'talk' to one another, producing a collaborative intelligence she described as 'forest wisdom'. Some older trees even 'nurture' smaller trees that they recognise as their 'kin', acting as 'mothers'. Seen in the light of Simard's research, the whole vision of a forest ecology shimmered and shifted – from a fierce free market to something more like a community with a socialist system of resource redistribution.'

A pandemic, climate change, a culture in which the economic imperative takes priority over humanitarian imperatives. Could this be the time to learn from nature and to rebuild the web of life which embraces the interdependence of humans and the natural world?

A REFLECTIVE BRICOLAGE

'Bricolage' is used by French anthropologist Claude Lévi-Strauss in *The Savage Mind* to describe the characteristic patterns of what he calls 'mythical thought'. In his description it is opposed to the engineer's creative thinking, which proceeds by asking a question and trying to design an optimal, if not complete, solution. Mythical thought, according to Lévi-Strauss, attempts to re-use random materials (bits and pieces, odds and ends, bric-a-brac), in order to solve new problems and present a range of perspectives.

Claude Lévi-Strauss, *The Savage Mind*

(THE UNIVERSITY OF CHICAGO PRESS, 1968).

The way in which the writing of this collection of lived experiences has developed over time, originated in a desire to present it as something of a bricolage. This desire arose from my reflections, occasioned by the trip to Shetland in May 2017, on how best to present a lived experience. In retrospect, it seemed to me that expectation and realisation merged to create the lived experience. So the record of the lived experience was in fact created before, during and after the event, as a concatenation of imaginings, memories and references to reading, together with various other sources. It is unlike history because it is not factual, but like history in that it is explanatory.

There is an extent then, to which this bricolage approach permeates much of the writing throughout PART ONE and PART TWO, but nowhere as much as in the reflections which close these lived experiences. The reason for this is that the concept of bricolage, while with me throughout the writing process, is only used explicitly following a serendipitously elegant coincidence, when I came across Meredith Monk's *On Behalf Of Nature*.

'I had been reading and thinking about ecology, climate change and how art could address these concerns. Believing in the universal healing power of music and that it speaks more directly than words, I worked to make a piece that had space for imagination and a fluid, perceptual field that could expand awareness of what we are in danger of losing. *On Behalf Of Nature* is a meditation on our intimate connection to nature, its inner structures, the fragility of its ecology and our interdependence. As I began working on the music for *On Behalf Of Nature*, I asked myself the question: "How would one make an ecological art work, one that didn't make more waste in the world?" What came to mind was the French anthropologist, Claude Levi-Strauss, and his notion of "bricolage": the process of assembling or making something from what is already at hand.'

Meredith Monk, *On Behalf Of Nature*

(CD, ECM, New Series, Munchen, 2016).

I saw this as such a felicitous coincidence, that I decided, rather than attempting to arrive at a conclusion through a process of reasoning and summing up, to offer some reflections on a bricolage of my thinking, and the thinking that has had an impact upon me, in the process of recording these lived experiences.

INTO THE CORE OF NATURE

'From that time forth he believed that the wise man is one who never sets himself apart from other living things, whether they have speech or not, and in later years he strove long to learn what can be learned, in silence, from the eyes of animals, the flight of birds, the great slow gestures of trees.'

Ursula Le Guin, *A Wizard of Earthsea*, The Earthsea Quartet, p.82

(Penguin Books, London, 2012).

'In nature we never see anything isolated, but everything in connection with something else which is before it, beside it, under it and over it.'

Johann Wolfgang von Goethe, *Maxims and Reflections,* translated by Elisabeth Stopp

(Penguin Classics, London, 1998).

The German word, *waldeinsamkeit*, refers to having a connection with nature, and enjoying time alone amongst it. Goethe was a writer and iconic figure of German Romanticism. 'It was his commitment to the revitalization of our perception of the world so that we again find ourselves at home within nature instead of studying her as if we were aliens from another planet that is his major contribution to science and, more broadly, to our beleaguered scientific culture today….. As conceived by Goethe, science is as much an inner path of spiritual development as it is a discipline aimed at accumulating knowledge of the physical world … From a Goethean standpoint, the ecological crisis is above all a crisis of our relationship to nature ….. His scientific path is a path which keeps faith with human experience, and seeks less to move from experience to idea or theory, than to intensify experience as such. It is through this intensification of our experience of nature that her spiritual dimension is revealed.'

Jeremy Naydler, *Goethe on Science*

(FLORIS BOOKS, EDINBURGH, 1996).

'The rippling cascades, sparkling arpeggios and reflective pauses' of Sarah Louise's guitar playing on her 2015 album, *Field Guide*, are described as 'evoking a precious sanctuary' of 'lyrical streams, dappled glades and bountiful forest floors'.

Deeper Woods (2018), another of Sarah Louise's albums, evokes and lyrically intertwines 'Appalachian flora and fauna' and their reciprocity with the 'emotional landscape' of the writer and performer. These songs of the land, and the land itself are, in Sarah Louise's view, the expression of an ancient consciousness which has been 'suppressed by capitalism, the patriarchy and white supremacy.'

Abi Bliss, *Cosmic Guitars*

(THE WIRE, 438, P.42, AUGUST 2020).

This perception of the natural world as a gift, abundant with music and teeming with poetry is not very far removed from the pastoral utopia of *As You Like It*:

'And this our life, exempt from public haunt,
Finds tongues in trees, books in the running brooks,
Sermons in stones, and good in everything.'

William Shakespeare, *As You Like It*, 2.1.15-17

(THE ARDEN SHAKESPEARE, LONDON, 2006).

'..... always roaming with a hungry heart
....
I am a part of all that I have met;
Yet all experience is an arch wherethrough
Gleams that untravelled world, whose margin fades
For ever and for ever when I move.'

Alfred Lord Tennyson, *Ulysses*, The Works of Tennyson

(MACMILLAN & CO., LONDON, 1926).

COMMODIFICATION

'What I see most of all are the adverts.....Everywhere an image, a phrase, a demand or a recommendation, is screaming for my attention, trying to sell me something, tell me who to be, what to desire and to need. And this is before the internet ...... before the deep immersion of people in their technologies, even outdoors, even in the sunshine.....this world is so tamed, so mediated and commoditised, that something within it seems to have been broken off and lost between the slabs .....The new world is online, and loving it, the virtual happily edging out the actual.'

Paul Kingsnorth, *Confessions of a Recovering Environmentalist*, p.65 & p.67

(FABER & FABER, LONDON, 2017).

'That smooth-faced gentleman, tickling commodity,
Commodity, the bias of the world.'

William Shakespeare, *King John*, 2.1.583-4

(THE RSC SHAKESPEARE, MACMILLAN, BASINGSTOKE, 2012).

'All of life now presents itself as an immense accumulation of
spectacles ...... All that once was directly lived has become mere
representation.'

Debord saw 'essential' social life replaced by its representation: 'the decline
of *being* into *having*, and *having* into merely *appearing*.'
    In Debord's view this condition of commodification, is the
'historical moment at which the commodity completes its colonisation
of social life.'

Guy Debord, *The Society of the Spectacle*

(BLACK & RED, KALAMAZOO, MICHIGAN, 1970).

Tony Harris points out in a Guardian article that Debord is 'talking about
alienation, the commodification of almost every aspect of life and the
profound social sea-change whereby any notion of the authentic becomes
almost impossible.'

Tony Harris, *Guy Debord Predicted Our Distracted Society*

(THE GUARDIAN FRIDAY, 30TH MARCH, 2012).

'Distracted from distraction by distraction
Filled with fancies and empty of meaning.'

TS Eliot, *Burnt Norton, III*

(FOUR QUARTETS, FABER & FABER, LONDON, 2001).

'The world comes at us minute by minute, day by day.... so that as
individuals we are always in danger of losing trust in our resourceful
selves, of falling under the wheels of the media machine, going dull

and dopey in domestic seclusion, losing detachment, forgetting that we have a stake in the ore of our selfhood and negotiating instead in the coin of the moment, the currency of the ephemeral. In this situation, poetry and art and cultural memory kick in like an emergency power system to reinforce the self, besieged as it is by this constant clamour and distraction of circumstance. They help the individual to credit the validity of personal experience and intuition.'

Seamus Heaney, *Room to Rhyme*, from The Great Minds Lecture

(University of Dundee, 2004.)

'Many of us need to remind ourselves to 'unplug,' to select the isolation knob, so that we might be present in the moment, or simply alone, and this is no easy task. For some, disconnection induces anxiety, a fear of missing out, a sense of isolation. So whilst hyperconnectivity is isolating in the way that it denies direct, personal experience, we have to isolate ourselves even further just to get away from it. It's an absurd paradox.'

Emily Buchanan, '*Only connect'? Forsterian ideology in an age of hyperconnectivity*

(Humanist Life, April 9th 2014).

APPOLONIAN, relating to the rational, ordered and self-disciplined aspects of human nature.

DIONYSIAN, relating to the sensual, intuitive and emotional aspects of human nature.

'Apollo, the god of light, of reason, of proportion, harmony, number – Apollo blinds those who press too close in worship. Don't look straight at the sun, go into a dark bar for a bit and have a beer with Dionysus, every now and then.'

Ursula K. Le Guin, *The Left Hand of Darkness*, Introduction, xv-xvi

(Gollancz, 2017).

FORESTS
ARE **NOT**
<u>COMMODITIES!</u>

The photograph of a placard held up at a demonstration caught my eye. It was particularly interesting to me as although it finishes with an exclamation mark it also contains questions. What are forests? What are they for?

> 'Now I was my body but I was also what my body walked upon. I was the grasses all of the different grasses and I was the peat of the moor and I was the heather and the skylark I had heard and I was the thing in the lane and these were not ideas they were not concepts they were not thoughts this was just how it was. I was everything. Here and now I was everything that was and had been and I was everything to come…
> ..Everything led up to me and everything I was would lead beyond me there was this great chain and I was a link in it. The past and the future they were nothing they were together and parted again and everything was rising and falling and swirling around everything else.'

Paul Kingsnorth, *Beast* pp.92-93

(Faber & Faber, London, 2017).

There was something of these sensations in my Bardsey Pilgrim experience. The week spent on Bardsey Island was probably the earliest instance of withdrawal in my experience. This was not into isolation but into something akin to total immersion in the natural world. First of all was the return to the sea, which, since the age of seven, when I first found my sea legs in coble perched on waves house-high, pitched, tossed and lifted while I taught the land stand still, captaining the deep, has been my true 'luminous home of waters':

From dryness deliver me, place me proud in the prow, with water's cloak, cloak me, cleanse me and heal me, spray me and soak me. It has occurred to me more than once that these lines, written after radiotherapy treatment (irradiation of the head and neck) which left me with xerostomia (dry

154

mouth), and other 'collateral damage' had a therapeutic essence to them. As at sea so on land, the connection with the natural world experienced on Bardsey Island both satisfied and stimulated: Lying on the heather, bracken fronds unfurling, ravens roll, chough dance, gulls glide, the sea hisses, I am spindrift, wind-borne, will o' the wisp. All enters me. I enter all.

FROM UTOPIA TO DYSTOPIA

'i am on a boat and now i see some distant coastline but there are no gapless lines of trees along the shore there are no clouds of birds bursting from the green and screeching into the sky ….. someone found this place centuries ago and built a city here and now it's all neon and glass and contrails and rainbow slicks of diesel I am alone circling the world through oceans of plastic …..'

Paul Kingsnorth, *Beast*, p.135

(FABER & FABER, LONDON, 2017).

Isle De Plastique

Jettisoned from ship or shore,
only a little piece of plastic,
a drop in the ocean, but just watch it grow
where currents converge and waters upwell,
where organic food and those who feed upon it
gather into the greatness of a widening gyre.

And in these widths the seen
and the unseen growing,
the first a raft the size of Texas
or bigger, or smaller, or more quiet
or still, a wonder of the world;
the second, what lies beneath,
a subtext of microplastics,
miniscule and microscopic,
these things so marvellous,
in their way.

'A few years ago, I went for a walk at Sissinghurst in Kent, a place I have loved all my life, and took with me a friend, Claire Spottiswoode, an ornithologist now working at the universities in Capetown and Cambridge, but who was brought up in Africa and has spent her life documenting the birds of that still-enriched continent. After a while in the heavy summer woods and fields, I turned to her and asked what she thought of this place, expecting her to love its deep and rooted beauty, the shadows of its oakwoods, the glow and burnish of its summer meadows. 'There is nothing here,' she said. 'Where is everything? Where are the animals? Where are the birds? It is empty. Everything has gone.'

Adam Nicolson, *The Seabird's Cry* p.352

(WILLIAM COLLINS, LONDON, 2017).

In the family home at fourteen years of age in the early sixties I recall one particular book, along with a few others such as *Dr In the House* and collections of Reader's Digest stories. *Silent Spring* was the book, Rachel Carson the author. This is a book which helped me at an early age to learn at least a little about the reckless use of pesticides, and the resultant damage to the natural world which primarily affects animals. Subsequently I came across the poetry of RS Thomas, and particularly his creation of the unstoppable mythical 'Machine' which stands for 'the industrial-technological-capitalistic-utilitarian-consumerist environment in which we attempt to live and move, attempt to communicate and attempt to have our being.'

Rachel Carson, *Silent Spring*

(HOUGHTON MIFFLIN, BOSTON,1962).

John G. McEllhenney, *A Masterwork of Doubting-Belief: RS Thomas and His Poetry*

(WIPF AND STOCK, OREGON, 2013).

Reviewing a biography of RS Thomas, Theodore Dalrymple suggests that this Welsh priest and poet's protestations at the way in which the worship of wealth and the growing reliance upon the machine was a constant throughout his adult life, raise a deep and unanswered question: 'What is life for? Is it simply to consume more and more, and divert ourselves with ever more elaborate entertainments and gadgetry? What will this do to our souls?'

> 'The world is too much with us; late and soon,
> Getting and spending, we lay waste our powers;
> Little we see in Nature that is ours;
> We have given our hearts away, a sordid boon!
> This Sea that bares her bosom to the moon;
> The winds that will be howling at all hours,
> And are up-gathered now like sleeping flowers,
> For this, for everything, we are out of tune;
> It moves us not.—Great God! I'd rather be
> A pagan suckled in a creed outworn;
> So might I, standing on this pleasant lea,
> Have glimpses that would make me less forlorn;
> Have sight of Proteus rising from the sea;
> Or hear old Triton blow his wreathèd horn.'

William Wordsworth, *The world is too much with us; late and soon,* *Selected Poems*

(PENGUIN CLASSICS, 2004).

BIOPHILIA

Biophilia is love of the natural world of which we are part. As Paul Kingsnorth puts it, 'We are all bound up together.....Then they – we – grow up to learn to convince themselves that 'objective' reality is somehow different from lived experience. We learn to convince ourselves that the world is a machine, not an animal, that it is unconscious and meaningless and that the only questions to be asked are questions of *how* and not *why* or *whether*' (p.56). Kingsnorth goes on to argue that we have created a culture in which many are 'alienated from the rest of life.' This so-called freedom has penned the majority of the population 'into cities where the stars of the night sky are obliterated by light pollution' and the air polluted by a combination of industrial emissions, fossil fuels and farming chemicals, with 'technological gadgetry' as the only compensation. 'Humans are animals – undomesticated animals – and there is something in us that still yearns for what Thomas Berry called 'the great conversation' (p.56) between humans and the rest of the natural world.

GREED

It may be dismissed as superstition or a misguided value system with its roots in popular religion but it is worth giving pause to Hindu belief in the concept of four different ages or 'yugas.' According to them the age we are currently living in is the 'Kali yuga, a dark age characterized by degeneration and greed' (p.57). Kingsnorth goes on to explain how avarice and a general disrespect for life define the Kali yuga: 'it is the age when humans have been telling themselves that they are equal to the gods for so long that they begin to believe it and act on it, with catastrophic consequences.' (p.57). Whatever the case I find it difficult to see any god other than Mammon being worshipped in practice. Aspiration for self rather than others, lack of fellow feeling, the rise of poverty for many and the wealth of the few, the prevalence of food banks and the ubiquitous hard-sell and must-have elements in advertising, are just some of the contributing factors and outcomes of greed.

WILDING

'If an unexamined yearning to reconnect with the wild world remains with us, then perhaps we will never quite allow ourselves to be tamed. It is a delicious thought that what might save us, in the end, will not be a new economic arrangement or a new politics or another revolution or a series of wonder technologies, but our own inner wildness, pushed under so hard and for so long that it finally bursts to the surface again, hungry for what it has lost.' (p.57).

Paul Kingsnorth, *Confessions of a Recovering Environmentalist*

(Faber & Faber, London, 2017).

AN OUTSIDER'S VIEW

'I've often thought that had I been compelled to live in the trunk of a dead tree, with nothing to do but gaze up at the patch of sky just overhead, I'd have got used to it by degrees. I'd have learnt to watch for the passing of birds or drifting clouds, as I had come to watch for my lawyer's odd neckties, or, in another world, to wait patiently till Sunday for a spell of lovemaking with Marie. Well, here anyhow, I wasn't penned in a hollow tree-trunk. There were others in the world worse off than I was. I remembered it had been one of Mother's pet ideas – she was always voicing it – that in the long run one gets used to anything.'

Albert Camus, *The Outsider*, pp. 79-80

(Penguin Books, Harmondsworth, 1973).

THE SOCIALIST POPE

"Pope Francis says the coronavirus pandemic has proven that the 'magic theories' of market capitalism have failed and that the world needs a new type of politics that promotes dialogue and solidarity, and rejects war at all costs. He laid out his vision for a post-COVID world by uniting the core elements of his social teachings into a new encyclical, 'Fratelli Tutti', Brothers All, which was released on the feast day of his namesake, the peace-loving mystic and patron of animals and the natural environment, St. Francis of Assisi."

This seems to me completely reasonable. Who would object to such humanitarian aspirations? Such a change from material aspirations. Interestingly, the desire for such a 'brave new world' draws its inspiration from the teachings of St. Francis and the pope's previous preaching on, 'the injustices of the global economy and its destruction of the planet, and pairs them with his call for greater human solidarity to address today's problems.'

"He said the pandemic, however, had confirmed his belief that current political and economic institutions must be reformed to address the legitimate needs of the people most harmed by the coronavirus. 'Aside from the differing ways that various countries responded to the crisis, their inability to work together became quite evident,' Francis wrote. 'Anyone who thinks that the only lesson to be learned was the need to improve what we were already doing, or to refine existing systems and regulations, is denying reality. 'He cited the grave loss of millions of jobs as a result of the virus as evidence of the need for politicians to listen to popular movements, unions and marginalized groups and to craft more just social and economic policies."

"'The fragility of world systems in the face of the pandemic has demonstrated that not everything can be resolved by market freedom,' he wrote. 'It is imperative to have a proactive economic policy' directed at 'promoting an economy that favours 'productive diversity and business creativity' and makes it possible for jobs to be 'created, and not cut.' He denounced populist politics that seek to demonize and isolate, and called for a 'culture of encounter' that promotes dialogue, solidarity and a sincere effort at working for the common good. As an outgrowth of that Francis repeated his criticism of the 'perverse' global economic system, which he said consistently keeps the poor on the margins while enriching the few. Francis rejected the concept of an absolute right to property for individuals, stressing instead the 'social purpose' and common good that must come from sharing the Earth's resources."

Nicole Winfield, Associated Press. 'Fratelli Tutti', Brothers All, Pope's encyclical, a collection of principles to guide Catholic teaching

(5ᵀᴴ OCTOBER, 2020).

THE NATURAL WORLD NOW

'It has been established beyond dispute that capitalism's assault on the environment is the driver behind the evolution of Covid-19 and other infectious diseases. Yet deforestation, pollution and land degradation continue at alarming rates.

The Global Virome Project estimates that there are 1.6 million unknown viruses circulating in wild animals, half of which have the potential of jumping to humans – a phenomenon known as zoonosis. The alarming increase in the number and frequency of zoonotic disease outbreaks correlates with the rapid transformation of forests, grasslands and deserts into urban and agricultural land. Discoveries published in

Nature on 5th August reveal that not only does habitat destruction increase the frequency of contact between humans and wildlife, it also makes it more likely for viruses to thrive.

According to the National Institute for Space Research in Brazil deforestation of the Brazilian Amazon increased by more than 50% in the first three months of 2020 in comparison to the previous year's first quarter.'

Bjork Lind, Revolutionary Communist Group, *Imperialism, a Breeding Ground for Pandemics*

(19TH OCTOBER, 2020)

HAROLD BLOOM'S IMMORTALITY

'When I saw Harold over the summer he started to tell me about a new book he wanted to write called *Immortality, Resurrection, Redemption: A Study in Speculation*. It was to be an exploration of the way people have imagined and hoped for something more or different once this life ends. It moved me that an eighty-nine-year-old writer and former teacher would spend whatever time was left wrestling with the very thing that would take him.'

As he subsequently wrote: *At ninety I have died and been resurrected five or six times. I refer to the many falls and grave illnesses that led to serious and successful surgery. My body—such as it is—is the Resurrection Body. I would interpret this as meaning that immortality is this life and so is redemption.*

'What did he know? Immortality is *this* life. So deepen it, live it profoundly. Harold may have been divisive, and he had his blind spots. But he taught us to live with characters, to think the world through writers, to see reality textured by literature: richer, more alive, redeemed. Because of Harold, I consider Falstaff an intimate friend—what he did, how he lived, his gift for presentness. Being with Harold always felt historic, momentous. The world around him was thick with thoughts and feelings, dense. The people we encounter in writing pierce us, their inner lives give us more life. For those of us who were lucky enough to study with him, Harold let that life out. And on mortality? As he liked to say, quoting Hamlet':

'If it be now, tis not to come, if it be not to come, it will be now; if it be not now, yet it will come. The readiness is all.'

Dear Lucas,

Does the world grow better or worse, or does it just get older? There is nothing new under the sun. Cultivating deep inwardness depends upon the reading of the world's masterpieces of literary works and religious scriptures. Not that Silicon Valley would be at all interested, but I would prescribe that all of them learn to read Shakespeare as he needs to be read. Self and soul would then return and take the place of fashionable evasions of the contingencies that have always shaped human lives.

Much of Freud is now obsolete but not his moral suggestion that we must all of us make friends with the necessity of dying. And yet, throughout the world, one form or another of spiritual hope affects the consciousness of moving inexorably towards death.

My prime interest is in our common human nature. Montaigne charmingly remarked that we need not prepare because, when the time came, we would know how to die well enough. But you and I are not Montaigne nor Shakespeare. We are curious, apprehensive, and would like to know more.

Love Harold

Lucas Zwirner, *Harold Bloom's Immortality*

(*FROM* THE PARIS REVIEW, OCTOBER 16TH 2019).

'Fires are raging in forests around the globe. You've probably seen the devastating photos of climate-fuelled wildfires in California. But did you also hear about Argentina, Australia... and the Arctic? And in the most important forest area of them all – the Amazon and other South American forests – fires have become such a predictable event that you can almost set your watch by it. Why? Because these fires are set deliberately as part of the destructive process of producing industrial meat. Areas of forest are slashed and burned and replaced with cattle farms and soya plantations. That same soya is used for animal feed on industrial farms here in the UK.'

(*FROM* A GREENPEACE PETITION REQUEST, 2020).

'What is the late November doing
With the disturbance of the spring
And creatures of the summer heat
And snowdrops writhing under feet
And hollyhocks that aim too high
Red into grey and tumble down
Late roses filled with early snow.'

TS Eliot, *East Coker*, Four Quartets

(FABER & FABER, LONDON, 2001).

Nel mezzo del cammin di nostra vita
mi ritrovai per una selva oscura,
ché la diritta via era smarrita.

'Midway upon the journey of our life
I found myself within a forest dark,
For the straightforward pathway had been lost.'

Dante Alighieri, *Inferno*, Canto 1, 1-3

'But the 21st century needs Sun Ra as well. Amid racial violence,
encroaching fascism and ecological emergency, he provides a path – not
out of, or through, but beyond the pressures of this moment.'

Matthew Blackwell. *The Wire*, 440, p. 80

(OCTOBER 2020).

'I have learned
To look on nature, not as in the hour
Of thoughtless youth; but hearing often-times
The still, sad music of humanity,
Nor harsh nor grating, though of ample power
To chasten and subdue. And I have felt
A presence that disturbs me with the joy
Of elevated thoughts; a sense sublime
Of something far more deeply interfused,
Whose dwelling is the light of setting suns,
And the round ocean and the living air,
And the blue sky, and in the mind of man:
A motion and a spirit, that impels
All thinking things, all objects of all thought,
And rolls through all things.'

William Wordsworth, from *Lines Written a Few Miles Above Tintern Abbey*, Palgrave's Golden Treasury

(OXFORD UNIVERSITY PRESS, 1966)

THE ECONOMICS OF BIODIVERSITY: THE DASGUPTA REVIEW

As biodiversity continues to disappear from our rivers, lakes and other wetlands, WWT welcomes the findings of the Dasgupta Review, the much anticipated assessment into the economics of preserving nature.

Until recently the link between environmental loss and economic decline had yet to take centre stage. However, the Review, the conclusions of which are launched today on World Wetlands Day, led by Professor Sir Partha Dasgupta, highlights the intrinsic importance of a sustainable and healthy economy built on the protection of our most important asset – nature.

The Review makes clear that human wealth depends on nature's health. It states that urgent and transformative action taken now would be significantly less costly than delay, and calls for change on three broad fronts.

- Humanity must ensure its demands on nature do not exceed its sustainable supply and must increase the global supply of natural assets relative to their current level. For example, expanding and improving management of protected areas; increasing investment in Nature-based Solutions; and deploying policies that discourage damaging forms of consumption and production.
- We should adopt different metrics for measuring economic success and move towards an inclusive measure of wealth that accounts for the benefits from investing in natural assets and helps to make clear the trade-offs between investments in different assets. Introducing natural capital into national accounting systems is a critical step.
- We must transform our institutions and systems – particularly finance and education – to enable these changes and sustain them for future generations. For example, by increasing public and private financial flows that enhance our natural assets and decrease those that degrade them; and by empowering citizens to make informed choices and demand change, including by firmly establishing the natural world in education policy.

As the world fights a pandemic amid nature, climate and well-being crises, WWT is calling for fundamental reform of our economic models, and for large-scale, healthy wetland restoration to be at the heart of realising Dasgupta's aims to preserve natural capital and boost prosperity.

Wildfowl and Wetlands Trust e-mail

(2ND FEBRUARY, 2021).

KOYAANISQATSI

The Hopi word is used in the film of that name to mean:
Crazy Life;
Life In Turmoil;
Life Disintegrating;
Life Out Of balance;
A State Of Life That Calls For Another Way Of Living.

Film Director: Godfrey Reggio, Music: Philip Glass, Cinematography: Ron Fricke

(ISLAND ALIVE FILMS, 1982).

NOTES

2   *Bocca Della Verita, made famous by the William Wyler film*: William Wyler, *Roman Holiday*, (DVD, Paramount Pictures, Los Angeles, 1953).

4   *the sea roads and islands of The Old Ways*: Robert Macfarlane, *The Old Ways*, pp. 87-138, (Penguin, London, 2012).
something of an Elysian lockdown: Elysian refers to a blissful place or feeling. It is derived from the Ancient Greek concept of the Elysian Fields, the place to which heroes were taken by the gods after death.

5   *my Days of Heaven*: Terrence Malick, *Days of Heaven*, (DVD, Paramount Pictures, Los Angeles, 1978). Although first seen well after the event which brought it to mind there is a particular resonance in Linda Manz's improvised narration of events as a streetwise orphan.

6   *the melancholy Jacques, living the Seven Ages of Man*: William Shakespeare, *As You Like It*, 2.7.140-167, (The Arden Shakespeare, London, 2006).
Oberon, who knew 'a bank where the wild thyme blows': William Shakespeare, *A Midsummer Night's Dream*, 2.1. 249-256, (The Oxford Shakespeare, 2008).

7   *'a beakerful of the warm South ..... with beaded bubbles winking at the brim'*: John Keats, *Ode to a Nightingale*. Keats' Poetical Works, (Oxford University Press, 1967).
played tennis with Miss Joan Hunter Dunn: John Betjeman, *A Subaltern's Love Song*, John Betjeman's Collected Poems, (John Murray, London, 1970).
He took us to Eliot's Waste Land: T. S. Eliot, Selected Poems, (Faber & Faber, London, 1967).
'the reek of buttoned carriage cloth': Philip Larkin, *The Whitsun Weddings*, (Faber & Faber, London, 1971).

11   *out of Ashes and Diamonds ..... my song is sung*: Andrzej Wajda, *Ashes and Diamonds*, (DVD, Paramount Pictures, Los Angeles, 1958). A film that made a considerable impact on my developing value and belief system during the sixties.

15   *like Hil and Bill up to the minute in brushtail possum*: Hillary and Bill Clinton were reputedly occasional wearers of fur-coats harvested from the brushtail possum. Evidently this was 'eco-fur'.

16   *a print of Vosper's Salem hanging above the fire*: The painting by Sidney Curnow Vosper (1908) is famous as a depiction of Welsh piety so it is something of an irony that some believe the devil to be depicted within it. It may be an example of pareidolia, cf. Shakespeare:

> Sometime we see a cloud that's dragonish,
> A vapour sometime like a bear or lion
> A towered citadel, a pendant rock,

A forked mountain, or blue promontory
With trees upon it that nod unto the world
And mocks our eyes with air.

Anthony and Cleopatra, 4.15.2-7
(The Oxford Shakespeare, 2008).

17   *'Breathless with adoration'*: William Wordsworth, from *It is a Beauteous Evening, Calm and Free.* Palgrave's Golden Treasury, (Oxford University Press, 1966).

20   *'Infinite Variety'*: William Shakespeare, *Anthony and Cleopatra*, 2.2.243, (The Oxford Shakespeare, 2008).

21   *as in the present moment of the morning we saunter south*: 'saunter' is from the French sans terre, a contraction of a la sainte terre, meaning 'to the sacred place,' i.e. 'a walking pilgrimage.'

22   *test for firm footholds, 'make our road by walking.'* Antonio Machado, *Campos de Castilla*, A Dual-Language Book edited & translated by Stanley Applebaum, (Dover Publications, Mineola, New York, 2017). This appears to be the origin of the concept of 'the road is made by walking'. A translation may help illuminate the resonance of the reference: 'Wanderer, your footsteps are the road, and nothing more; wanderer, there is no road, the road is made by walking. By walking one makes the road, and upon glancing behind one sees the path that never will be trod again. Wanderer, there is no road – Only wakes upon the sea.'

23   *All of The Usual Suspects in attendance*: *The Usual Suspects*, Brian Singer, (DVD, Polygram, Beverly Hills, CAL, 1995).
     'To the Lighthouse': Virginia Woolf, (Vintage Classics, London, 2004).

26   *'Who is it that can tell me who I am?'* William Shakespeare, *King Lear*, Scene 4, 222, (The Oxford Shakespeare, 2008).
     'One equal music': John Donne, *Our Last Awakening*, Prayer Resource, St Matthew's, London.
     Rhoda, Jinny, Louis, Bernard, Susan and Neville are six characters who are, judging by the way Virginia Woolf investigates the nature of their identity, definitely not in need of an author. Virginia Woolf, *The Waves*, (Penguin Classics, London, 2011).
     'the good minute goes': Robert Browning, from *Two in the Campagna*. Browning: A Selection by W.E. Williams, (Penguin Books, Harmondsworth, 1966).
     'the present moment' is a concept valorised in, among others, the writing of Epicurus, Johann Wolfgang von Goethe, Rainer Maria Rilke, George Eliot and Virginia Woolf.
     'the divine specific': Virginia Woolf, *The Waves*, (Penguin Classics, London, 2011).
     fragments to shore against her ruin is a line derived from *'these fragments I have shored against my ruins'*: TS Eliot, *The Waste Land*, Selected Poems, (Faber & Faber, London, 1967).

'in the foul rag-and-bone shop of the heart': W.B. Yeats, *The Circus Animals Desertion*, W.B. Yeats Selected Poetry, (Macmillan, London, 1967).

'moments of being': Virginia Woolf, *Moments of Being*, Edited by Jeanne Schulkind, (Random House, New York, 2002).

A collection of autobiographical writings by Virginia Woolf. Woolf describes these phenomena as moments in which an individual experiences a heightened sense of reality, in contrast to the states of 'non-being' that dominate most of an individual's conscious life in which they are separated from this heightened sense of reality by 'a kind of nondescript cotton wool.'

30   *gather samphire on cliffs*: this is a reference to 'Halfway down, / Hangs one that gathers samphire': William Shakespeare, *King Lear*, Scene 20,15, (The Oxford Shakespeare, 2008).

31   *'the skull beneath the skin'*: T.S. Eliot, *Whispers of Immortality*, Selected Poems, (Faber & Faber, London, 1967). The phrase is used in the poem as a reference to John Webster's being 'much possessed by death.'

I cannot eat my dinner: To fit my personal circumstance this is an adaptation of Caliban's *'I must eat my dinner'*: William Shakespeare, *The Tempest*, 1.2.331, (The Arden Shakespeare, London, 2011).

'this island's mine': William Shakespeare, *The Tempest*, 1.2. 332, (The Arden Shakespeare, London, 2011).

32   *'I would have broke mine eye-strings, cracked them'*: William Shakespeare, *Cymbeline*, 1.3.17, (The Oxford Shakespeare, 2008).

37   *A splendidly glossy, black rock hen, as gracious and beautiful as Pertelote*: Pertelote was the favourite 'wife' of the rooster Chanticleer in Chaucer's cautionary and satirical, Nun's Priest's Tale.

39   *Ultima Thule*: Virgil, Georgics 1. 30. The term was coined by Virgil to mean 'furthest land,' a symbolic reference to denote a far-off land or an unattainable goal.

maalie: Shetland name for the fulmar.

alamootie: Shetland name for the storm petrel.

bonxie: Shetland name for the great skua.

40   *tammie norie*: Shetland name for the puffin.

41   *'Kindness is the golden chain by which society is bound together'*: Johann Wolfgang von Goethe, *Maxims and Reflections*, Translated by Elisabeth Stopp, (Penguin Classics, London, 1998).

44   *'luminous home of waters'*: Matthew Arnold, l.890, *Sohrab and Rustum*, The Oxford Book of Narrative Verse, (Oxford University Press, 1989).

And the beer is from the Valhalla brewery: Valhalla is the majestic hall for heroes ruled over by Odin and to which supernatural beings, the Valkyries, deliver them.

46   *Kveldsro*: (kel-dro), Old Norse for 'evening peace.'

47   *'To lead life heedlessly, without reserve, entirely given over to the magic of the moment'*:
Stendhal, *The Charterhouse of Parma*, (Oxford World's Classics, 2009).
*'Seven Days, that were connected/Just like I expected, they'd be coming on forth /My beautiful
comrades from the north.'*: Bob Dylan, *Seven Days*, The Bootleg Series, Volume 3,
(CD, Columbia Records, New York, 1991).

48   *in the company of that man of mystery, Nostromo*: Joseph Conrad, *Nostromo*, (Penguin
Classics, London, 2007).

49   *The Lady of Shalott*: Alfred, Lord Tennyson, Palgrave's Golden Treasury, (Oxford
University Press,1966). A lyrical ballad about a young noblewoman isolated in a
tower but determined to participate in the living world rather than a world
reflected in a 'mirror blue.'
Simeon Stylites on his pillar: An ascetic who wished to escape from society, so lived
on a platform on top of a pillar. Coincidentally this is also the subject of a poem
by Tennyson.

50   *'Solitary in the field, senses sharpened. To sit and wait brings one into Harmony with the pulse
of the day'*: John Busby, *Birds in Mallorca*:(Helm Field Guides, London,1988).
Santuari de Lluc: A monastery and site of a pilgrimage, founded in the thirteenth
century, in the Tramuntana mountains.

51   *'The splendour falls on castle walls'*: Alfred, Lord Tennyson, Palgrave's Golden
Treasury, (Oxford University Press,1966).
This is something of a musical paean to nature, the glory of the past and the
Romantic imagination. It has the resonance of the free expression of feelings of
Caspar David Friedrich's, *Wanderer above the Sea of Fog* (about which, as Friedrich
said, 'The artist's feeling is his law.') It's interesting to note that Delius, Vaughan
Williams, and Britten all set the words to music.

53   *'These pleasant places were once, for me, a sweet invitation to write'*: Ludovico Ariosto,
Satire IV. This is from one of the Seven Satires written during the years between
1517 and 1525 to relatives and friends. It evinces a calm, confidential and self-
analytical approach not usually associated with satire. His wit lies not in
invective or 'preachiness' but in affability.
'The untold want by life and land ne'er granted, Now, Voyager, sail thou forth, to seek and find':
Walt Whitman, *Leaves of Grass*, (1855 edition, Penguin Classics, London, 2005).

54   *'Nature, red in tooth and claw'*: Alfred, Lord Tennyson, *In Memoriam* (W.W. Norton &
Company, London, 2003).

55   *throughout the voyage the sea state never became worse than Slight or Moderate.*
The ten sea states are as follows: Calm (glassy); Calm (rippled); Smooth
(wavelets); Slight; Moderate; Rough; Very rough; High; Very high; Phenomenal.

storm petrels: The storm petrel is a bird I have wanted to see, and perhaps *be*, from the age of ten. Its habitat has always been something with which I could readily identify as my preferred environment or natural home. *'The open sea, coming to land only at night to nest on marine islands; hardly ever in inshore waters, and inland only as a storm-blown waif':* R.S.R. Fitter & R.A. Richardson, *Pocket Guide to British Birds,* (Collins, London,1959).

56 *'No creatures made so mean, But that some way, it boasts, could we investigate, Its momentary task, gets glory all its own, Tastes triumph in the world, pre-eminent, alone.'* Browning, R. (1872) *Fifine at the Fair* Kessinger's Rare Reprints, Whitefish, Montana, (2004).

57 *'The petrel and the porpoise ... on the vast waters':* T.S. Eliot, *Four Quartets, East Coker V, 37-38* (Faber & Faber, London, 2001).

58 *'Sometimes looking at the fulmar's gaping, mouth-opening, mutually frenzied, head-bobbing':* Adam Nicolson, *The Seabird's Cry,* (William Collins, London, 2017).

60 *'the lonesome corncrake's cry of sorrow and delight':* The Pogues, *Lullaby of London,* If I Should Fall from Grace with God, (CD, Warner Music, New York, 1988).

61 *'When thou seest an Eagle, thou seest a portion of Genius; lift up thy head!':* William Blake Poems, *The Proverbs of Hell* pp. 37- 40 (Faber & Faber, London 2010).
'Old men ought to be explorers / Here or there does not matter': T.S. Eliot, *Four Quartets,* East Coker, V,31-38, (Faber & Faber, London, 2001).

62 *Carpe Diem:* An aphorism attributed to the Roman poet, Horace, (Odes, 23 BC) and meaning seize the day. Robin Williams used the words in role as the inspirational English teacher in *Dead Poets' Society* (1989): 'Carpe diem, boys! Seize the day. Make your lives extraordinary!'
'Every day there's one less day to seize': Salman Rushdie, *The Moor's Last Sigh,* (Vintage Classics, London,1995).
'Morning Has Broken' is a Christian hymn, written by Eleanor Farjeon, hymnary.org/text/morning_has_broken, 1931.
Lyonesse: A country in Arthurian legend, supposedly on the western edge of Cornwall, and, according to Mediaeval Celtic tales, said to have gradually become a land lost beneath the waves, thus connecting it both physically and mythically with the Isles of Scilly.

63 *'It is a beauteous evening, calm and free': William Wordsworth,* from the sonnet of that title. (See Note 17 above).
'Play me a song, Mr. Wolfman Jack': Bob Dylan, Murder Most Foul (CD, Columbia Records, New York, 2020).
'Anywhere I lay my head': Tom Waits, Rain Dogs (CD, Island Records, London,1985).

64   '*That's the wise thrush; he sings each song twice over*': Robert Browning, Home
      Thoughts, From Abroad. Browning: A Selection by W.E. Williams, (Penguin
      Books, Harmondsworth, 1966).

69   '*Daisies are our silver, buttercups our gold: This is all the treasure we can have or hold.*
      Raindrops are our diamonds And the morning dew; While for shining sapphires We've the
      speedwell blue.' Jan Struther, hymnary.org/text/daisies_are_our_silver, 1935.
      '*And Moses stretched out his hand over the sea; and the Lord caused the*
      Sea to go back by a strong east wind all that night, and made the sea dry
      land, and the waters were divided': The Bible, Exodus 14:21, King James *Version*.

70   Alfred Watkins, *The Old Straight Track*, (Little, Brown Book Group, New
      York,1988).
      Look, stranger, on this island now': W.H. Auden, On This Island, Collected Shorter
      Poems, (Faber & Faber, London, 1969).

71   '*Embrace the Butcher*': Bertolt Brecht, The Measures Taken and other Lehrstücke
      (Methuen Drama, Bloomsbury, 2015).

72   *Herodotus*: The inscription on New York City's GPO building is a reference to the
      courier service of the ancient Persian Empire, taken from a translation of
      Herodotus' Histories, (430BC?).

73   '*The Infant St John and the Lamb*': Bartolome Esteban Murillo, The painting
      depicts John the Baptist as a child, with a lamb symbolic of Christ, (1645?).

74   '*brave new world*': William Shakespeare, *The Tempest*, 5.1.183, (The Arden
      Shakespeare, London, 2011). Aldous Huxley used *Brave New World* as the title of
      his dystopian novel of 1932. As well as using the title he also used many
      quotations from the play in the themes and ideas of the novel.

76   *the oak eggar moth, the first of many, and later the subject of much discussion* about Terence
      Stamp and Samantha Eggar: The association motivating the discussion was a
      William Wyler film, The Collector (1965), in which Terence Stamp plays a
      lepidopterist who kidnaps a beautiful art student, Samantha Eggar.

77   '*hurl and gliding' rebuffing the 'big wind*': The Windhover, Gerard Manley Hopkins,
      Poems and Prose, (Penguin Books, Harmondsworth, 1966).

79   *the ring of a fantasy novel by Alan Garner*: Alan Garner, *The Weirdstone of Brisingamen*
      (William Collins, Glasgow, 1960). This novel, in fact all of Garner's writing, has
      a significant connection with the themes and ideas explored throughout these
      lived experiences in that these experiences, like much of Garner's work,
      frequently embrace the concept of a 'Living Landscape', or, more in the spirit of
      Romanticism, what Paul Kingsnorth conceptualises as, 'the notion of a sensate
      landscape'.

82   *'drink life to the lees'*: Alfred Lord Tennyson, *Ulysses*, The Works of Tennyson, (Macmillan & Co., London, 1926).
'hungry heart': This is also from Tennyson's *Ulysses*, and the title of a Bruce Springsteen song from the 1980 album, *The River.*
Captain Cuttle's advice, 'When found, make a note of it': Charles Dickens, *Dombey and Son*, (The Educational Book Co. Ltd., London, 1910).

83   *scribbly jacks*: A popular north eastern name for yellow hammers, taken from the characteristic scribbled patterning on their eggs.
'young and easy': Dylan Thomas, *Fern Hill*, Collected Poems 1934-1953, (J.M.Dent, London, 1996).
'gave delight and hurt not': William Shakespeare, *The Tempest, 3.2.136*, (The Arden Shakespeare, London, 2011).

84   *this empty space in this 'brave new world'*: As with Miranda's utterance 'O brave new world / that hath such people in't', on seeing a group of unknown humans, my usage of the term 'brave new world', from Shakespeare's *The Tempest*, is intended to carry some potential irony and a suggestion of the unknown future.

85   *'or just another song that's in my heart to linger on?'*: *Tomorrow Night, written by* Sam Coslow & Will Grosz, Bob Dylan, Good As I Been To You, (CD, Columbia Records, New York, 1992).

89   *another striking reminder of Browning's astute observation which I applied earlier to the common skua or bonxy*: See PART ONE, A DREAM OF ISLANDS, p. 56 and note.
I'm in the purlieus of Ternelles watching some creature with a talent for singing like some croaking, laughing birds: See PART ONE, A DREAM OF ISLANDS, p.51.

90   *'Then heaven blazes in my breast'*: The experience brings to mind Judith Weir's musical composition *Heaven Ablaze in His Breast*, based on Hoffman's, *The Sandman*, for the dance company, Second Stride in 1989.

93   *The truly, telling moment of 'being there'*: C.W. Watson (Ed.), Being There: Fieldwork in Anthropology, (Pluto Press, London, 1999).
Territorial Imperative: Robert Ardrey, (Atheneum, New York, 1966).

94   *Mirabile dictu, he flies toward me, then directly over my head*: mirabile dictu, a Latin phrase with the sense, 'wonderful to relate.'

95   *'Thousands of the almost fluorescent arachnids have been terrifying Brits across the country'*: Levi Winchester, Daily Express, (Wednesday, June 10, 2015).

96   *'The Bliss of Solitude'*: William Wordsworth, Palgrave's Golden Treasury, (Oxford University Press, 1966).
'For solitude sometimes is best society': John Milton, *Paradise Lost* IX, 249, (Oxford University Press, 2005).
'Ravel's Bolero': Maurice Ravel, (CD Deutsche Grammophon, Berlin,1966).

98   *A climb accompanied by The Boss singing Keep Your Eyes on the Prize:* Bruce Springsteen
We Shall Overcome: The Seeger Sessions (CD, Columbia Records, New York,
2006). Bruce Springsteen is popularly known as 'The Boss.' Keep Your Eyes on
the Prize was an anthem for the Civil Rights Movement of the 1950s and 60s,
based on the traditional song *Gospel Plow.*

102   *The 'golden wings of fame':* William Shakespeare, *King Edward III, (1.47)* (The
Arden Shakespeare, London, 2017).
whisk me back to my flight of fancy with Basher Grey: The concatenation of events
factual and fictional (PART ONE, A DREAM OF ISLANDS, pp.7-8) owe their
gestation and realisation to the infectious enthusiasm of a teacher whose love of
Shakespeare has continued to inspire since 1965.

103   *The most comprehensive version of the myth of Philomela, Tereus and Procne is in Ovid's
Metamorphoses, Book VI:* On the way to Athens with her escort, King Tereus of
Thrace, Philomela is raped by the king. Following her threat to tell her story to
everyone, Tereus cuts out her tongue. Regarding herself as blameless, she weaves
a robe with her story so that Procne, the wife of Tereus, learns of the event. After
further attempts at revenge all three are changed into birds by the Olympian
gods. Tereus a hoopoe, Procne a swallow and Philomela a nightingale.

104   *Like Vosper's Salem or Anthony's clouds an example perhaps of pareidolia:* See PART
ONE, A DREAM OF ISLANDS, p.16 and note.
'Dylan's Murder Most Foul & I Contain Multitudes': Rough and Rowdy Ways (CD,
Columbia Records, New York, 2020).
'The Courage of Others': Midlake, (CD, Bella Union, London, 2010).

105   *The Wild Flowers of the Malvern Hills,* Keith Barnett, (The Self Publishing
Association Ltd., Hanley Swan,1991).
In a moment of being we see one another: See last note on p. 26, PART ONE, A
DREAM OF ISLANDS

106   *Just been reading the Introduction to Edward III with Richard Proudfoot and Nicola Bennett
doing an excellent job:* The editors of William Shakespeare, *King Edward III,* (The
Arden Shakespeare, London, 2017).
'nil desperandum Young Chambers': The encouraging words of Mr Felton, a young
history teacher, making his path through life.

107   *a company of Red Legs:* Clint Eastwood, *The Outlaw Josey Wales,* (DVD, Warner
Bros., Hollywood, CAL, DVD, 1976).

108   *the opening shot of Mr Turner':* Mike Leigh, *Mr Turner,*(DVD, Sony Pictures, London,
2015).
*'Sunk for a long time in profound thoughts – Shakespeare must have written like that, and the
church builders built like that':* Virginia Woolf, *Orlando,* p.101, (Oxford World's
Classics, 2008).

109 '*My Day's Plan to Write*': Kathleen Raine, Selected Poems, (Golgonooza Press, Ipswich, 1988).

110 *Dylan Thomas' Fern Hill*, The Collected Poems, (JM Dent, London, 1996).

111 '*The Usual Suspects*', Brian Singer, (DVD, Polygram, Beverly Hills, CAL, 1995). A notably different group to 'the usual suspects' of Bardsey Island.

113 *Kathleen Jamie, from Findings*, Fever, p.109, (Sort Of Books, London, 2005). *One of Jacky's favourite gospel songs comes in on the ocean swell of association.* The Charioteers, *Wade in the Water*, (1940). *Beginners Guide to Gospel, CD 1*, (Old Time Religion: Gospel Roots, Nascente Series, 2004)

115 '*Joy, bright spark of divinity, / Daughter of Elysium, / Drunk with fire we tread / Within thy sanctuary / Thy magic power re-unites / All that custom has divided / All men become brothers, / Under the sway of thy gentle wings*': Friedrich Schiller, Ode to Joy.

116 '*the bead-bonny ash*': Gerard Manley Hopkins, *Inversnaid*, Poems and Prose, (Penguin Books, Harmondsworth, 1966).

117 *Lauded by Alex and his Droogs as the Glorious Ninth*: Anthony Burgess, *A Clockwork Orange*, (Penguin Modern Classics, London,1962).

118 *the music shines 'brighter than a thousand suns'*: the phrase comes from the Bhagavad Gita and is said to have been uttered by J. Robert Oppenheimer at the Trinity nuclear test. It was later used as the title to a book about the scientists who developed the first atomic bombs.
'Gladly! Just as His suns hurtle/ Through the glorious universe, / So you, brothers, should run your course, / Joyfully, like a conquering hero': Friedrich Schiller, Ode to Joy.
a group of heathland reserves within the Wyre Forest which have been identified as a priority in Worcestershire's 'Living Landscapes' approach: The 'Living Landscapes' approach is both a local and a national initiative for the Wildlife Trust.

119 '*Me, no good boyo, up to no good in the wash-house*': Dylan Thomas, *Under Milk Wood and Other Plays*, (Audiobooks CD, Naxos, United Kingdom, 1954).

120 '*at the still point of the turning world*': TS Eliot, *Burnt Norton II*, Four Quartets, Faber & Faber, London, 2001).
'*The Pylons*': Stephen Spender, Poetry of the Thirties, (Penguin, Harmondsworth, 1971).
'*You are the music while the music lasts*': TS Eliot, *The Dry Salvages V,* Four Quartets, Faber & Faber, London, 2001). 'For most of us, there is only the unattended / Moment, the moment in and out of time, The distraction fit, lost in a shaft of sunlight, / The wild thyme unseen, or the winter lightning / Or the waterfall, or music heard so deeply / That it is not heard at all, but you are the music / While the music lasts.' The essence here is 'being in the present moment', focussing attention away from thoughts of past and future.

121 *'aspens dear, whose airy cages quelled or quenched in leaves the leaping sun'*: Gerard Manley Hopkins, *Binsey Poplars*, Poems and Prose, (Penguin Books, Harmondsworth, 1966). *taking me for a moment to the fig in 'Women in Love'*: DH Lawrence, (Oxford University Press, 1998).

122 *the quivering lips and trembling facial expression of Vanessa Redgrave*: Fred Zinnemann, *A Man For All Seasons*, (DVD, Columbia Pictures, Los Angeles, CAL,1966). *Jan Struther's 'shining sapphires'*: See note for p. 69, PART ONE, A DREAM OF ISLANDS.

123 *'The Keepsake'*: Samuel Taylor Coleridge, Selected Poems of S.T. Coleridge (Heinemann Books Ltd, London, 1968).
'Annihilating all that's made / To a green thought in a green shade': Andrew Marvell, *The Garden*, The Complete Poems, (Penguin Classics, London, 1996).
I recall Lear coming into contact with the plight of the poor and homeless: William Shakespeare, *King Lear*, Scene 11, 25-30, (The Oxford Shakespeare, 2008). The words of the speech resonate with empathy and fellow-feeling in what is for Lear a Road to Damascus experience.

124 *Such temporal disintegration, occurs in Thomas Mann's narrative in 'The Magic Mountain' where Hans Castorp finds shelter during a snow storm:* Thomas Mann, *The Magic Mountain*, (Vintage Classics, London, 1999).

125 *a sheet of barren blue for the alouettes to fertilise with their song*: While the word 'alouette' is French for lark it is not in common usage for the skylark in Britain. The name comes from my childhood memory of singing the French-Canadian song about plucking the feathers from a lark: 'Alouette, gentille alouette, Alouette, je te plumerai.'

126 *'Our minds wander' she says, explaining that they are 'responding to sensory stimulants in nature'*: Nicola Chester, *Nature's Home*, (Autumn / Winter 2020).
Buddy Holly, *Take Your Time*, 1956, Coral Records, USA, (Vocalion, 1967).

127 https://en.wikipedia.org/wiki/Xanthoria_parietina

128 *'the male drums on the web to announce he is calling'*: Britain's *Wildlife, Plants & Flowers*, (Reader's Digest Association, London, 2002).
'beauty truly blent': William Shakespeare, *Twelfth Night*, I.5. 231, (The Arden Shakespeare, London, 2008).

129 *'In a somer seson / Whan softe was the sonne …. Werchynge and wandrynge / As the world asketh'*: Extract from The Project Gutenberg EBook of Langland, W. *The Vision and Creed of Piers Plowman* Ed. Thomas Wright (1887). Release date, September 2013.

134 *'Weave a circle round him thrice, And close your eyes with holy dread, For he on honey-dew hath fed, And drunk the milk of Paradise.'*: Samuel Taylor Coleridge, *Kubla Khan*, Selected Poems of S.T. Coleridge, (Heinemann Books Ltd, London, 1968).

135 *unlike the Murillo painting I admired in the Church of the Holy Spirit on the Isle of Wight*: See PART ONE, A DREAM OF ISLANDS, p. 73 and note.
didappers: another name for the dabchick or little grebe.

136 *'insatiate cormorant'*: William Shakespeare, Richard II, 2.1.38, (The Oxford Shakespeare, 2011).
more Golgotha or Gesthemane than Eden or Avalon: See PART ONE, A DREAM OF ISLANDS, p. 22.
'Slough of Despond': John Bunyan, *The Pilgrim's Progress,*(Harper Press, London, 2013).

137 *ringing with some remembered resonance of the same yellow colour scheme back on the Isle of Wight:* See PART ONE, A DREAM OF ISLANDS, penultimate paragraph on p. 78.
'In my end is my beginning': TS Eliot, *Four Quartets,* East Coker, V, (Faber & Faber, London, 2001).
Today The Waste Land, 'dry sterile thunder without rain': TS Eliot, *The Waste Land,* What the Thunder Said, V, 342, (Faber & Faber, 1967).

138 ACHOO (Autosomal Dominant Compelling Helio-Ophthalmic Outburst). Colloquially sun sneeze, or the photic sneeze reflex.

139 *one of the keys to the vision of a 'Living Landscape'*: the WWT network of habitats stretching across town and country that allow wildlife to move about freely and enable people to enjoy the benefits of nature.

140 *'danced their ringlets to the whistling wind'*: William Shakespeare, *A Midsummer Night's Dream,* 2.1.86, (The Oxford Shakespeare, 2008).
where 'Jack Orion' curses 'oak and ash and bitter thorn': Pentangle, *Jack Orion*, Cruel Sister, (CD, Sanctuary Records, Surrey, 1970).

141 *where Shelley shouts 'if winter comes, can spring be far behind?'*: Percy Bysshe Shelley, *Ode to the West Wind,* Palgrave's Golden Treasury, (Oxford University Press,1966).
and Bert Jansch sings of 'springtime promises': Pentangle, *Basket of Light,* (CD, Sanctuary Records, Surrey, 1969).
Baroness Orczy's scarlet pimpernel: This is a plant which can be found throughout Europe, so in one sense is not so 'damned elusive' as the hero of Baroness Orczy's novel. It could, however, be said to be elusive in another sense in that its flowers close in mid-afternoon and are always shut during dull or wet weather.

142 *the disintegrating carapaces remind me of the cracking and bursting seed pods of spring*: See p.116, ODE TO JOY, middle paragraph.

143 *'You shall not think 'the past is finished' Or 'the future is before us'*: The Dry Salvages, TS Eliot, *Four Quartets,* (Faber & Faber, London, 2001).
'Time past and time future What might have been and what has been Point to one end, which is always present': Burnt Norton, TS Eliot, *Four Quartets,* (Faber & Faber, London, 2001).

144 *'There is a crack, a crack in everything, That's how the light gets in'*: Leonard Cohen, Anthem, The Future, (CD, Columbia, Los Angeles, 1992).

145 *An extended family of long-tailed tits, bumbarrels as John Clare called them*: Emmonsail's Heath in Winter, John Clare, Selected Poems, (JM Dent& Sons Ltd.1975).
Richard Thompson (Keep Your Distance): Rumor and Sigh, (CD, Capitol Records, Los Angeles, 1991). The title of the album comes from an Archibald MacLeish poem, 'Rumor and sigh of unimagined seas/Dim radiance of stars that never flamed.'
The Police (Don't Stand So Close To Me): Zenyattà Mondatta, (CD, A&M Records, Santa Monica, 1980).

146 *'Elgar's Nimrod'*: Edward Elgar, Enigma Variations, (CD, EMI Classics, London, 1991). The ninth movement in the variations is known as Nimrod, after Elgar's friend August Jaeger, whose surname is German for hunter. This reference also embraces Nimrod as the powerful hunter figure of the Bible. It has some further resonance in that it suggests a rebellious spirit, not unfamiliar in these parlous and potentially turbulent times.
'Dance No. 3, Philip Glass': Dance Nos. 1-5, (CD, Sony Music, New York, 1980).

147 *'For centuries, fungi had generally been considered harmful to plants; parasites that caused disease and dysfunction'*: Robert Macfarlane, *Underland*, p.89, (Hamish Hamilton, UK, 2019).
Simard termed 'an underground social network': Simard in Robert Macfarlane, *Underland*, p.89, (Hamish Hamilton, UK, 2019).
'Instead of seeing trees as individual agents competing for resources, she proposed the forest as a 'co-operative system' .... Seen in the light of Simard's research, the whole vision of a forest ecology shimmered and shifted – from a fierce free market to something more like a community with a socialist system of resource redistribution': Robert Macfarlane, *Underland*, pp.90-91, (Hamish Hamilton, UK, 2019).

ACKNOWLEDGEMENTS

It has never escaped my notice that much of this record of the lived experiences of *Journeys* was written in the context of a global lockdown that was far from Elysian for the vast majority of people. The hardships and profound suffering of so many, together with the loss of jobs and lives, sits uneasily next to what is essentially celebratory writing, and I trust my efforts to avoid feelings of solipsism are successful.

My thanks go to Derek Paget for his assiduous reading of the first completed draft of what became *Journeys*. Once a colleague, now a close friend, who provided responses and asked questions which proved invaluable in contributing to the final shaping of this book.

Margaret Vernon and Lyndon Knott have helped to open up the natural world for me in many different ways. I hope that they can see *Journeys* as an expression of my appreciation of their efforts.

For written feedback on *Journeys* thanks go to Sharon Zink of Jericho Writers and to Phil Box. For verbal feedback during the course of its writing I thank Sam Chambers, Jacky Chambers, Tod Chambers, Dil Porter and Kirtee Bhosekar. For their support, encouragement and belief in my writing endeavours thanks go to my sister, Kathryn Hopps and my aunt, Marilyn Garcia. My cousin Pam Armstrong I thank for our shared appreciation of ecstasy and the present moment in literature and the natural world. To my long-time friend Dave Holt thanks are due for walks, and discussions on numerous subjects which helped in the shaping of *Journeys*.

There are others whose presence I felt during the writing process. My mother. Basher Grey. My cousin John Vickers, who was there at the beginning. And all of the following who have helped me notice while out in the field: Sheila Jones, Vanessa Chaplin, Jane Campbell, Nick Skilbeck, Richard Newton, Cherry Greenway, Charles Robertson, Caroline Robertson, Alan Baxter, Susie Kimber, Geraldine Guppy, Mike Hails, Brian Stretch, Janet Jones, Paul Edlin, Helen Tudge, Mike Sheridan, Melanie Bell, Heather Hayward, Roger Hayles, Marcela Hayles, Phil Hitchen, Cameron Badenoch, Kathy Badenoch, Sandra Young, Carol Newton, Maggie Reed, Martin Reed, Roy Finch, Frances Finch and Brian Harding.

For many kinds of help on the journey I thank Alan Robertson, Alan Robinson, Brian Clarke, Tony Redding, Helen Flanagan, Geraldine O'Gara, George Hudson, Swaroop Rawal, Hilde Stroobants and Shaun Hughes.

My special thanks go to Vince Russel for his prompt and unassailable help in the solving of technological mysteries, and to Ruby Chopra and Lisa Dowdeswell of The Society of Authors for their efficiency and clarity in dealing with matters of copyright in relation to Virginia Woolf. Finally, thanks are due to Adrian Sysum for his sterling work on preparing *Journeys* for publication, and to Rachel Woodman, Editorial & Production Manager of The Choir Press, for her patience and good humour throughout the publishing process.

Lightning Source UK Ltd.
Milton Keynes UK
UKHW011947190122
397397UK00003B/72